Making Connections

Making Connections

Case Studies for
Student-Centered Classroom Assessment,
Second Edition

Kathleen U. Busick
and
Richard J. Stiggins

Assessment Training Institute, Inc.

Project Coordination and Editing: Carolyn M. Buan Writing & Editing Services
Project Assistant: Nancy Bridgeford
Production: Jennifer Dickey
Design and Typesetting: Irish Setter

1998 Second Printing

Printed in the U.S.A.

ISBN 0-9655101-0-7

Library of Congress Catalog Card Number 96-79211

Additional copies of this book may be ordered from the Assessment Training Institute. Discounts are offered for bulk orders. Call 503-228-3060 or 800-480-3060.

To the children of the Pacific islands

Table of Contents

Acknowledgments   xi

Introduction: Using Cases with *Student-Centered Classroom Assessment*, Second Edition   1

Chapter 1   A Principled View of Assessment   9

Case 1.1   The Challenge of Dealing with the Media   9

Case 1.2   A Community's Dilemma About What Constitutes a "Good School"   10

Chapter 2   Understanding the Critical Role of Assessment   13

Case 2.1   The Dilemma of Differing Assessment Purposes   13

Case 2.2   The Changing Role of Standards and Classroom Assessment   15

Case 2.3   Assessing Special Needs Students   16

Chapter 3   Specifying Achievement Targets   19

Case 3.1   Name the Graph: What Are We Looking For?   19

Case 3.2   What in the World Is "Creative Problem Solving"? Defining an Elusive Target   20

Case 3.3   How Do We Build Common Meaning? Defining Habits of Mind   22

Case 3.4   Developing Multiple Criteria   24

Chapter 4   **Understanding All of the Assessment Alternatives**   27

Case 4.1   A Debate About Appropriate Ways of Assessing   27

Case 4.2   The Dilemma of Defining Complex Learning   28

Case 4.3   The Case of the Restrictive Policy   32

Chapter 5   **Facing the Barriers to Quality Assessment**   35

Case 5.1   When Can I Go to the Bathroom? The Barrier of Time   35

Case 5.2   Chickens and Pigs: Language That Inhibits Assessment   37

Case 5.3   "This Too Shall Pass." The Teacher Who Is Set in His Ways   38

Chapter 6   **Selected-Response Assessment**   41

Case 6.1   The Dilemma of Multiple-Choice Test Bias   41

Case 6.2   The Challenge of Fixing a Troubled Test   42

Case 6.3   Matching Exercises and Thinking Across Languages   46

Case 6.4   Focusing on Important Learning: What's Worth Assessing?   48

Chapter 7   **Essay Assessment: Vast Untapped Potential**   51

Case 7.1   The Case of the Surprising Essay Assessment   51

Case 7.2   What Does Quality Look Like? The Dilemma of Conflicting Communication Patterns   53

Case 7.3   Developing Multiple Criteria Revisited   54

Case 7.4   Accounting for More: What's the Match Between the Task and the Criteria?   55

Chapter 8   **Performance Assessment: Rich with Possibilities**   59

Case 8.1   A Term Paper Assignment   59

Case 8.2   A Science Application of Performance Assessment   61

Case 8.3   Seeking Quality Performance Criteria   62

Chapter 9   **Personal Communication: Another Window to Student Achievement**   65

Case 9.1   Assessing Inquiry: Can We Use Student Questions As Evidence of Learning?   65

Case 9.2   The Case for and against Participation Grades   66

Case 9.3   Evaluating Teacher Performance in the Area of
             Effective Questioning   67

Chapter 10   Assessing Reasoning   69

Case 10.1   The Dilemma of Multiple Targets   69

Case 10.2   Evaluating the Quality of Reasoning   71

Case 10.3   A Sound Assessment of Reasoning?   71

Case 10.4   Questioning to Learn vs. Questioning to Challenge   73

**Chapter 11   Performance Assessments of Skill and
                 Product Targets   77**

Case 11.1   Two for the Price of One? Assessing Reading
             and Writing Together   77

Case 11.2   Aligning Instruction and Assessment   81

Case 11.3   Criteria for Collaboration   84

Chapter 12   Assessing Student Dispositions   87

Case 12.1   Habits of Mind in the Arts: Do You Want Me to
             Tell You What You Think? Or Do You Want to
             Know What I Think?   87

Case 12.2   The Evaluation Committee   93

**Chapter 13   Classroom Perspectives on Standardized
                 Testing   95**

Case 13.1   The Problem of Textbook Selection   95

Case 13.2   The Confusing Standardized Test and Its Resulting
             Scores   96

Case 13.3   Kelly and the Reading Test   97

**Chapter 14   Understanding Our Communication
                 Challenge   103**

Case 14.1   "Incomplete" Grades Go Out of Control   103

Case 14.2   The Disappearing Motivation   104

**Chapter 15   Developing Sound Report Card Grading
                 Practices   107**

Case 15.1   The Dilemma of the Zero   107

Case 15.2   The Service Teacher's Dilemma   108

Case 15.3   The Stolen Answer Key   109

Chapter 16   **Using Portfolios as a Communication System**   111

Case 16.1   The Dilemma of Student Selection and Clear Communication   111

Case 16.2   Portfolio Reflections: How Do We Judge Quality?   113

Case 16.3   A Request from High Places   117

Chapter 17   **Tapping the Full Potential of Student-Involved Communication**   119

Case 17.1   The Special Needs Student Revisited   119

Case 17.2   The High School Faculty Debate on Student-Led Conferences   119

Case 17.3   The Failed Conference   121

Acknowledgments

As we prepared the cases in this book, we relied on many educators to tell us about assessment challenges they have experienced. Had they not permitted us to see the hurdles they face, we would not have been able to learn so many valuable lessons about quality classroom assessment. We sincerely appreciate their willingness to share their stories.

The teachers and parents represented in these cases strive to accommodate the needs of students from incredibly diverse cultures. Our understanding of the interaction of culture, language, and assessment—limited though it is—arises from their willingness to offer insights from their classrooms.

Although we wrote this book together, we also want to acknowledge some people who have been especially helpful to us individually.

Kathy has been privileged to work with extraordinary educators in Assessment Coaching groups throughout the Pacific region. She offers special thanks to the assessment coaches in American Samoa, the Marshall Islands, Pohnpei, Chuuk, and Yap State (where this work began) and to her training and coaching partner, Pamela Legdesog; to Carol Iacovelli for her thoughtful work engaging students in habits of mind; to Hawaii Literacy Hui; and to the teachers, parents, community, students, and staff of Waialae Elementary School, who allowed Kathy to learn with them as they struggled to create an assessment system that matched their powerful vision for students.

Rick thanks the hundreds of teachers and administrators from across the United States and Canada who have shared their classroom assessment dilemmas—many from their own perspectives as parents, too. Special thanks to Ken O'Conner of Scarborough, Ontario, Board of Education; Jay McTighe of the Maryland Assessment Consortiuim; Richard Paul of the Center for Critical Thinking, Santa Rosa, California; Vicki Spandel of the Northwest Regional Educational Laboratory, Portland, Oregon; Anne Davies of

Classroom Connections, Courtney, British Columbia; and the British Columbia Ministry of Education. All shared especially challenging cases and unique insights into solutions. All asked questions that deepened our own thinking.

Finally, we appreciate Nancy Bridgeford's excellent review and feedback as we wrote, Carolyn Buan's outstanding editorial contributions, and the diligent work of Jennifer Dickey and Sharon Lippert during manuscript preparation.

Introduction

USING CASE DISCUSSIONS WITH STUDENT-CENTERED CLASSROOM ASSESSMENT, *SECOND EDITION*

Throughout the *Student-Centered Classroom Assessment* text, readers are offered many opportunities to reflect on classroom assessment ideas in relation to their own personal classroom assessment experiences. This approach helps to build assessment literacy in individually relevant ways. The text (1) clarifies, expands, and integrates readers' knowledge about classroom assessment, (2) engages them in thoughtful reasoning about assessment issues and procedures, (3) helps them to become skillful in using the material presented—within their own professional contexts, and (4) encourages them to acquire the attitudes needed to develop and effectively use high-quality classroom assessments.

As a companion to the text, *Making Connections* serves those same purposes—but in a slightly different way. It calls for the careful application of ideas and strategies covered in the text to resolve very complex, real-world classroom assessment cases in which teachers face challenging dilemmas. Each case stimulates reflection, discussion, and the search for resolution. We collected these cases to provide practice for pre-service and in-service teachers and administrators in applying what they are learning.

What Is a "Case"?

Each case in *Making Connections* offers a glimpse into a real classroom assessment situation. Each presents a dilemma shared with us by practicing teachers and administrators out of their own personal professional experi-

1

ence. (All names have been changed and some circumstances slightly altered in deference to those who shared them with us.) We offer these cases for use in your professional development so you can continue the search for solutions that the educators who shared them struggled to find.

Typically, the cases are presented in three parts: (1) the description of the problem or dilemma, (2) suggestions for initial individual reflection, and (3) discussion starters or specific work assignments. Be sure to read the case very carefully before proceeding. Take time to reflect and collect your thoughts before analyzing and discussing it in depth. Try not to converge on a single solution or answer too quickly. Remain open to the range of possibilities.

Most of the dilemmas presented do not have "right" answers or magical keys to resolution. Several solutions may be viable. Therefore, we provide no answer key but leave it to you to dig into your own developing assessment literacy to figure out possible solutions. We expect that you will apply your learning in ways that spawn solutions we would never have thought of. If you do, you will be "making connections." This is our goal.

How Should Cases Be Used?

As your assessment literacy increases, so will your ability to resolve increasingly complex challenges. The *Student-Centered Classroom Assessment* text and this casebook are both organized to spiral you through increasingly sophisticated levels of understanding of the assessment process. So they offer increasingly complex challenges. For this reason, we strongly recommend that you use *Making Connections* right alongside the text. As you finish each text chapter, address one or more of its cases—just for practice. As you will see, some cases presented with early chapters appear again in later chapters. Your increasing assessment literacy will let you amplify your initial solutions and sense your own improvement. Thus, we model a kind of self-assessment you might use with your students to help them see and take responsibility for their own improvement.

An interesting variation on this idea involves selecting a few cases from the case book at random before you begin your study and seeing if you can solve them. Write down your initial solutions and—as you proceed through the text and apply new insights to those same cases—compare your early and later solutions. You should see concrete evidence of your own growth.

Whenever possible, we encourage you to form a study team to help you work through these cases. If the casebook is used in the context of graduate or undergraduate course work, the entire class can serve as the study team or can be subdivided into working teams. If the casebook is to be used in an in-service context, find colleagues interested in learning to solve real-world classroom assessment problems in effective ways. Remember, we know more collectively than any of us does individually, so we can learn by pooling our knowledge. Remember too that we reason more effectively when we use our collective problem-solving power. We encourage extensive group discussion as a means of resolving these case dilemmas, and we like teams comprised of both teachers and administrators.

What Is the Case Discussion Process Like?

The process of deliberating about and resolving cases is summarized in the following lists:

Expect Case Discussions Involving	**But Not**
Really difficult questions	Problems with transparent solutions
Collaborative reflection	Work in isolation
Solutions that evolve from reflection and discussion	Quick answers
Dilemmas with real consequences	Artificial, hypothetical situations
A challenging search for consensus	Automatic and complete agreement
The challenge of trying to fit "round" assessment concepts into "square" problems	An easy fit of methods to dilemmas
Analytical thinking leading to creative solutions	Rote recall of the text
Solutions that come from within	Solutions that come from some "authority"
The search for rich insight into student motivation and learning	Simplistic notions of student motivation
An opportunity to become your own change agent	Reliance on others to promote the effective use of quality classroom assessments
Students who take charge of their own academic well-being	Students who expect answers to come from someone else

How Do These Cases Fit into the Self-Assessment Process?

Case discussions afford an excellent opportunity for educators to experience, in our own self-assessments, those procedures we advocate as useful for our students. Your study of the *Student-Centered Classroom Assessment*, Second Edition text can be accompanied by any of a variety of such self-assessment experiences.

1. PERSONAL "TIMES FOR REFLECTION" DIARY. The text includes a continuous series of structured "Times for Reflection." Take time to write down your responses for later review and reflection.

2. END OF CHAPTER LEARNING EXERCISES FILE. Each chapter ends with practical application exercises. Commit to actually doing the work and recording your responses. Save these for later reflection.

3. STUDY TEAM LEARNING LOG. When the text is used in learning teams, each member can keep a personal log or you can take turns recording team meeting experiences. As you read and learn about the intricacies of classroom assessment, reflect on personal insights, breakthroughs, achievements, frustrations, and other reactions.

4. EXTENDED UNIT PROJECT PORTFOLIO. An extended assignment is woven through the chapters of the text calling for the design and development of assessments for a unit of instruction selected by the reader. Again, invest the time needed to do the work and collect the results.

5. PORTFOLIO OF CASE STUDY SOLUTIONS. As you complete the cases presented herein, chapter by chapter, assemble a portfolio of your (individual or learning team) solutions. From time to time, you can return to earlier solutions and use your ever-increasing assessment literacy to see new ways to approach the problems presented. Reflect on and write about your expanding knowledge and skills. Collect these self-reflections in your portfolio, too.

We can build a sense of personal accountability for our own professional development in assessment by allocating time for personal reports on our progress. We can develop and share portfolios and logs. At the end of your study, you should be ready to present compelling evidence that you are more competent as a classroom assessor than you were at the beginning.

Working With Clusters of Cases

While we recommend that you take up each case within the context of its related chapter in *Student-Centered Classroom Assessment*, Second Edition, it is also possible to select cases that have a common strand and organize your discussions around particular assessment issues. Here are some natural clusters for cases that appear in different chapters:

Following the Journey of a Single School

2.1 The Dilemma of Differing Assessment Purposes

3.2 What in the World is "Creative Problem Solving"? Defining an Elusive Target

5.1 When Can I Go to the Bathroom? The Barrier of Time

16.1 The Dilemma of Student Selection and Clear Communication

16.2 Portfolio Reflections: How Do We Judge Quality?

Engaging Parents and Community in Assessment Conversations

1.1 The Challenge of Dealing with the Media

1.2 A Community's Dilemma About What Constitutes a "Good School"

2.2 The Changing Role of Standards and Classroom Assessment

4.2 The Dilemma of Defining Complex Learning

4.3 The Case of the Restrictive Policy

5.3 "This Too Shall Pass." The Teacher Who Is Set in His Ways

14.2 The Disappearing Motivation

15.1 The Dilemma of the Zero

16.1 The Dilemma of Student Selection and Clear Communication

17.1 The Special Needs Student Revisited

17.2 The High School Faculty Debate on Student-Led Conferences

17.3 The Failed Conference

Culture, Language, and Assessment

3.1 Name the Graph: What Are We Looking For?

4.2 The Dilemma of Defining Complex Learning

5.2 Chickens and Pigs: Language that Inhibits Assessment

6.1 The Dilemma of Multiple-Choice Test Bias

6.3 Matching Exercises and Thinking Across Languages

7.1 The Case of the Surprising Essay Assessment

7.2 What Does Quality Look Like? The Dilemma of Conflicting Communication Patterns

9.2 The Case for and against Participation Grades

10.4 Questioning to Learn vs. Questioning to Challenge

Opportunities to Adapt or Repair Assessment Tasks and Criteria

3.1 Name the Graph: What Are We Looking for?

3.3 How Do We Build Common Meaning? Defining Habits of Mind

3.4 Developing Multiple Criteria

5.2 Chickens and Pigs: Language that Inhibits Assessment

6.2 The Challenge of Fixing a Troubled Test

6.4 Focusing on Important Learning: What's Worth Assessing?

7.3 Developing Multiple Criteria Revisited

7.4 Accounting for More: What's the Match Between the Task and the Criteria?

8.3 Seeking Quality Performance Criteria

10.1 The Dilemma of Multiple Targets

10.3 A Sound Assessment of Reasoning

11.1 Two for the Price of One? Assessing Reading and Writing Together

11.3 Criteria for Collaboration

12.1 Habits of Mind in the Arts: Do You Want Me to Tell You What You Think? Or Do You Want to Know What I Think?

16.2 Portfolio Reflections: How Do We Judge Quality?

System and Policy Decision Making

1.1 The Challenge of Dealing with the Media

1.2 A Community's Dilemma About What Constitutes a "Good School"

4.3 The Case of the Restrictive Policy

14.1 "Incomplete" Grades Go Out of Control

16.3 A Request from High Places

Assessment in the Arts and Service Areas

3.3 How Do We Build Common Meaning? Defining Habits of Mind

12.1 Habits of Mind in the Arts: Do You Want Me to Tell You What You Think? Or Do You Want to Know What I Think?

15.2 The Service Teacher's Dilemma

Assessing the Learning of Children with Special Needs

2.3 Assessing Special Needs Students

17.1 The Special Needs Student Revisited

Responding to Student Work—Describing Quality, Feeding Forward, Grading, and Reporting

3.3 How Do We Build Common Meaning? Defining Habits of Mind

4.3 The Case of the Restrictive Policy

7.1 The Case of the Surprising Essay Assessment

7.4 Accounting for More: What's the Match Between the Task and the Criteria?

12.1 Habits of Mind in the Arts: Do You Want Me to Tell You What You Think? Or Do You Want to Know What I Think?

14.1 "Incomplete" Grades Go Out of Control

15.1 The Dilemma of the Zero

15.2 The Service Teacher's Dilemma

15.3 The Stolen Answer Key

16.1 The Dilemma of Student Selection and Clear Communication

Focusing on Design and Technical Issues

6.2 The Challenge of Fixing a Troubled Test

6.3 Matching Exercises and Thinking Across Languages

7.3 Developing Multiple Criteria Revisited

7.4 Accounting for More: What's the Match Between the Task and the Criteria?

8.3 Seeking Quality Performance Criteria

Applying Assessment Quality Standards to Instructional Materials and Text-Embedded Assessments

12.2 The Evaluation Committee

13.1 The Problem of Textbook Selection

13.2 The Case of Confusing Standardized Test and Its Resulting Scores

Cases at the Elementary Level

2.1 The Dilemma of Differing Assessment Purposes

2.2 The Changing Role of Standards and Classroom Assessment

3.1 Name the Graph: What Are We Looking For?

3.2 What in the World Is "Creative Problem Solving"?

5.1 When Can I Go to the Bathroom? The Barrier of Time

6.2 The Challenge of Fixing a Troubled Test

11.3 Criteria for Collaboration

15.3 The Stolen Answer Key

16.1 The Dilemma of Student Selection and Clear Communication

17.3 The Failed Conference

Cases at the Secondary Level

1.1   The Challenge of Dealing with the Media

3.3   How Can We Build Common Meaning? Defining Habits of Mind

3.4   Developing Multiple Criteria

5.3   "This Too Shall Pass." The Teacher Who Is Set in His Ways

6.1   The Dilemma of Multiple-Choice Test Bias

6.3   Matching Exercises and Thinking Across Languages

7.1   The Case of the Surprising Essay Assessment

7.2   What Does Quality Look Like?

7.3   Developing Multiple Criteria Revisited

12.1   Habits of Mind in the Arts: Do You Want Me to Tell You What You Think? Or Do You Want to Know What I Think?

15.1   The Dilemma of the Zero

15.2   The Service Teacher's Dilemma

17.2   The High School Faculty Debate on Student-Led Conferences

1

A Principled View
of Assessment

1.1 THE CHALLENGE OF DEALING WITH THE MEDIA

Please reread the opening scenario of Chapter 1—the story of Emily and the school board meeting. When you have done so, please return to this case and read on.

A newspaper reporter was in attendance at that school board meeting. The next day, a story appeared in the local paper under the headline,"Local Students Fail Writing Test."

At the beginning of the article, he analyzes Emily's beginning-of-year (pretest) writing sample point by point according to its flaws. Then, in an example of balanced reporting, he points out that the author of this flawed piece demonstrated better writing skills later in the year, though he presents no evidence of improved skills.

As you read on, you find out why this particular reporter selected this headline. It was not because Emily had done poorly at the board meeting, for he acknowledges that she did very well. Rather, the reporter had two separate but related reasons for highlighting student failure.

First, he wanted to point out how inadequate Emily's writing instruction must have been before the tenth grade. What, he asks, had been going on in writing instruction in the elementary and middle schools to produce a writer so incapable of composing coherent text?

The reporter's second reason for complaining was more fundamental—the apparent narrowness of the new writing program at the high school. The only form of writing Emily had been taught to do well was narration—story telling and personal point of view. What, the reporter asks, about expository writing for use in business contexts, persuasive writing, and creative or poetic writing?

The entire tone of the article is quite negative, despite the extremely positive experience everyone had at last night's board meeting. The article just leaves you frustrated in many ways.

Initial Reflections

When you have finished the article, you are moved to communicate with three people in this order: Emily, the newspaper reporter, and a high school English teacher. Specifically, what would you say to each and why?

Before you answer the above question, think about these issues:

1. How well is each likely to understand what it means to be a good writer?
2. How much are they likely to know about quality assessment?
3. What kind of feedback from you is most likely to be productive from the recipient's point of view?
4. How can you employ your own assessment literacy to maximize your positive impact through your communication?

Discussion Starters

1. Starting with Emily, outline the key points you will make in your communication to each person.

1.2 A COMMUNITY'S DILEMMA ABOUT WHAT CONSTITUTES A "GOOD SCHOOL"

Overheard at last week's school board meeting:

Ms. Smith: "Mr. Superintendent, could you please tell the community why you're launching this school reform effort? What's wrong with schools the way they are? What's wrong with schools the way they were when we attended? We all seem to be doing all right, thank you very much. My desires are simple. Just provide me with a safe place to put my two girls every day— a place where I know they won't be attacked or get hurt. I just want to be sure someone is watching over them. I need to go to work every day confident that they'll be OK 'til I pick them up at 5:30. Do we need sweeping reforms to achieve this?"

Superintendent: "Ms. Smith, we are reforming schools because we need a different kind of graduate today than when we were in school. We need graduates who are competent—who can read to gain information and to do a job, write for the purposes of practical communication, use their knowledge to solve real-world problems, serve as productive members of a team. The schools we grew up in didn't teach us these things, Ms. Smith, and you know it. Effective schools produce competent graduates."

Mr. Alvarez: "But wait a minute, Mr. Superintendent, I've been hearing about this teamwork stuff. In our neighborhood, they're calling it cooperative learning. Everybody helps everybody—like a family. Look, we'll take care of family at home. That's not a school thing. It's a competitive world out there. Survival of the fittest. I competed in high school and won a scholarship. Because I won, someone else lost. That's the way it is. Dog eat dog. My kid is very bright and I want him to win. Keep him in a competitive school—where he doesn't have to help all of his opponents win too—and he'll finish at the top. He has a shot at becoming valedictorian. Just give us the same old rank order of students at the end of high school—that's an effective school."

Initial Reflections

Here we see three widely differing visions of what it means to provide a quality education: serve a custodial function, assure competence, and sort students from the highest to the lowest achiever. Analyze each vision according to these three questions:

1. What world view forms the basis of each speaker's opinion about quality schools? How does the schooling experience relate to real life for each of them?

2. What does it mean for an individual student to experience success in each case? By what standards do we judge the effectiveness of schools?

3. How would you measure the students' success in each case? What specific index or indices of academic success would tell you if schools are effective?

Discussion Starters

1. When you have completed your analysis of these visions of effective schools, discuss how a school district might reconcile the differences.

2. Is it possible to offer schooling experiences that are safe and competitive, while producing competent students?

3. What roles might the assessment process and its results play in the ongoing operation of such a school system?

2

Understanding the Critical Role of Assessment

2.1 THE DILEMMA OF DIFFERING ASSESSMENT PURPOSES

The newly appointed state superintendent of education has tied his job to increasing standardized test scores within three years. He's made it clear to school administrators that they must emphasize preparation for and improvement in grade-level scores. The superintendent has vowed that public school accountability will be his first priority and has recommended that test-taking strategies be given increased attention in classroom instruction.

While the superintendent has affirmed the importance of local decision making through school-community councils, he believes that classroom assessments vary so widely in quality that they cannot be used for accountability. He has challenged schools to show how they are preparing students for success on statewide tests.

Your school was a pioneer in community-school governance. Working together, teachers, parents, community members, school administration, and students crafted a vision for success that focuses on creative problem solving, self-confident risk taking, caring, and concern for others as well as acquisition of knowledge across disciplines. Two years ago, as part of local governance, your school received a waiver excusing it from statewide testing of young children on the condition the school demonstrate that a viable assessment system was in place to determine the strengths and needs of students. That evolving assessment system includes twice-yearly reading interviews at all grade levels, portfolios to document growth in problem solving and writing, an array of performance assessments for projects, and checklists for documenting skill development and behaviors.

In today's teachers' meeting, reaction to the superintendent's challenge is immediate. Third grade teachers express concern that their hard work is going to be pushed aside by renewed emphasis on large-scale standardized testing. These teachers have spent a lot of time defining the school vision in terms of important content, developing criteria with students, expanding assessment to include things like concept webbing, videotaping students in the midst of projects, doing other kinds of performance assessments, and experimenting with alternatives to traditional report cards.

One teacher worries that although progress has been made, the school's assessment system isn't yet ready to "go public." Her remark prompts a thoughtful question from a fourth grade teacher: "Do our current assessments give us really high-quality information about all of the things we value?"

A sixth grade teacher talks about her worry that the time necessary to continue developing and improving other forms of assessment is going to be consumed by preparing students for large-scale testing. A few years ago, she and her partner resisted changes in assessment. Now she cites changes in her own students that cannot be measured on standardized tests—changes in their initiative, the quality of their decision making, their persistence, and the kinds of questions they raise and seek to answer. She and her fellow sixth grade teachers believe these skills and dispositions are vitally important to the future success of their students.

Your school-community council meeting is coming up. The superintendent's statements are at the top of the agenda. Parents have been calling to check teachers' reactions and to wonder how this will affect the assessment system that teachers have been developing for the past four years. Some feel that the superintendent has articulated a concern of their own—the quality of classroom assessments—and reinforced their wish to know how well their children are doing compared to their classmates. Other parents have been eager participants in the search for alternatives and worry that the vision that had defined learning targets will be lost in pursuit of scores on tests that don't come close to providing a full picture of learning.

Initial Reflections

There are a number of questions for teachers and the council to wrestle with:

1. How should the council respond to the superintendent's position while remaining consistent with their school-community vision?

2. What arguments could be made for continuing the development of the school's assessment system?

3. How should the school-community define accountability?

4. Are there ways for the school to take part in statewide testing without losing time and energy for their own work on valued learning targets?

Discussion Starters

1. How would you advise them to proceed?

2.2 THE CHANGING ROLE OF STANDARDS AND CLASSROOM ASSESSMENT

At a recent local Parent-Teacher Association meeting about assessment, an elementary school principal presented information about changes that were under way. She spoke eloquently about the central role of assessment in promoting and portraying student learning. The evening included hands-on activities introducing parents to performance assessments that require the use of criteria and disciplined judgment about the quality of student work. Parents completed an assessment task similar to one recently used in fifth grade and entered into a lively discussion of the key characteristics of a quality response.

Toward the end of the evening, teachers shared a set of guiding beliefs about assessment that they had crafted together. Heads nodded around the room as statements echoed the beliefs and experiences of parents and school staff alike. Easy assent greeted statements like, *No one method of assessment can give information about achievement of the full range of learning objectives. Therefore a combination of different methods is vital if we are to get a balanced picture of student development.*

There was a shifting in the room, however, when another statement was read: *Assessment tasks should be designed so that most children in a group do well in most tasks. This takes the threat out of being assessed and allows children to be motivated to learn by the regular experience of success and praise.* The principal invited parents to comment and raise questions.

In the midst of a number of very positive comments, a parent asked whether using tasks that most students can do well wouldn't "dumb down" the curriculum—simplifying and reducing the demands on students to master challenging content. "Is making students feel motivated more important than preparing them for the future?" His concern was shared by others who asked for more information about this "new direction" in assessment. "Won't our children learn even less if everyone has to do well?"

This parent's view of the role of assessment was framed by the images of his own school experience—that a very few can be expected to do well, while a similarly small number will do very badly and most students will fall somewhere in the middle. The staff, however, has come to believe that effective tasks can involve significant intellectual challenge without dooming large numbers to failure.

Initial Reflections

1. Is this parent's fear justified?
2. Will de-emphasizing competition in assessment result in less challenging content? Under what circumstances? Can such problems be avoided?

Discussion Starters

1. Specifically, how should the school principal respond to this expression of concern?

2.3 ASSESSING SPECIAL NEEDS STUDENTS

A Mom talks about her special needs child:

"My Matthew has trouble with reading and writing because of his learning disability. His teachers say he's making progress. But I'm not sure. I really *want* to believe them—Matt's a good kid. He seems to try very hard. But it's so difficult for him—has been ever since first grade. He's in sixth grade now and I just don't know what to think.

"His grades seem OK, not great. Matt and I spend a lot of time on his homework. So I get to see firsthand every night how much trouble he has learning. I wonder what his teachers are evaluating that makes them think his achievement is improving. I wonder if they really know how Matt's doing.

"They give him quite a bit of homework to do. He and his teacher enter homework in his assignment journal at the end of each day. He brings it home, and every night right after dinner we begin working and continue until after 9 p.m. We work through one assignment at a time, step by step until he's done—often fighting tooth and nail as we go. Most of the time he seems to get it—finally. But things like vocabulary, spelling, or figuring out what words mean from a story's context don't seem to stick. He seems to have to relearn things over and over.

"Well, anyway, I make sure the work he takes back to school every morning is correct. I just wish he could make sure it is correct.

"We've received special education assistance ever since first grade. Every year his teachers and the whole special education staff work together to write Matthew's 'individual educational program.' Then they're supposed to see if he's reaching his objectives. But I never understand the results of their assessments at the end of the year. It's all so complicated, with test scores, grades, results of something they call 'classroom observations,' and the like. They always seem to be so encouraging, so supportive, so appreciative of my involvement. But Matthew doesn't seem to be learning. He can't do much of anything independently. He always needs to turn to me for help.

"Here's Matt's plan for this year for improving his reading and writing skills:

Objective	*Assessment Plan*
1. Read a passage and answer questions.	80% average on quarterly tests Classroom observation Observation of class assignments
2. Proofread his writing and edit for punctuation, grammar, usage, and spelling.	Same as above
3. Complete a class research project using library resources.	Same as above
4. Name and use resources available in resource room, texts, and computer lab.	Same as above

"I wish I could tell them to look at the things I see as Matt does his homework every night as part of this 'assessment plan.' But all I get when I talk with his classroom teacher and special education assistant is that they rely on 'classroom observation.' What is that anyway? And how do I know if we can trust it? It seems to me that I'm 'observing' something different from what they're observing."

Initial Reflections

1. Clearly, Matthew's mom is assessing his achievement and she's concerned. Do you think her assessments are of high quality? Why?
2. Similarly, Matt's teachers are assessing. What do you think about the quality of their assessment plan and their assessments?

Discussion Starters

1. Matt's mom sees a major discrepancy between the two assessments. To what might you attribute those differences?
2. If you were going to advise Matt's mom about how to proceed with the concerns she has expressed, what would you advise her to do?
3. What should she be doing at home in working with Matt?
4. What should she do within the context of her working relationship with Matt's teachers?

3

Specifying Achievement Targets

3.1 NAME THE GRAPH: WHAT ARE WE LOOKING FOR?

To help teachers better understand how opened-ended assessment exercises can give insights into student learning, a district science specialist decided to use a graph-based task and try it out with eighth grade students. He adapted a task that had been presented by an Australian educator at a regional conference. Originally used in mathematics, the task requires students to look at a bar graph with no labels, numbers, or title and create a story that accounts for the bars. The specialist wanted to add some directions for students to make it clear what constituted a quality response. Here's the pilot version of the exercise:[1]

> *Directions: <u>NAME THE GRAPH</u> is an activity that requires you to think creatively and remember important things that you learned in science in the past. There is no one right answer for this activity. Your score will be based on the following criteria:*
>
> *3 points*   *1. Naming the graph in relation to a science lesson you have learned in the past. Put names and numbers properly to show what you mean.*
>
> *5 points*   *2. Tell a good story about your graph. Write down everything you know from your graph (make connections as to why, what, when, how, etc.).*
>
> *2 points*   *3. The clarity of your work.*

Examining the results of the pilot, the specialist was disappointed. A new hands-on science curriculum was in its second year and a significant number of the teachers had received intensive training the previous summer. The specialist expected to have some strong examples from this pilot to share with newer teachers and to gradually move toward more performance-based assessments. With few exceptions, students responded with minimal information, and many missed some of the required elements. What went wrong?

Initial Reflections

1. What kind(s) of target(s) is the specialist aiming for?
2. On what basis might the students have been confused?

Discussion Starters

1. How could the specialist make his achievement expectations clearer?
2. How might the difficulties experienced by students in responding to this task have been avoided?
3. How would you suggest that the assessment be improved for the next round?

3.2   WHAT IN THE WORLD IS "CREATIVE PROBLEM SOLVING"? DEFINING AN ELUSIVE TARGET

Early in a district's move toward the creation of a student-centered school, parents, community, and teachers crafted a vision from their hopes and dreams for the future of their children. One of the key elements of that vision was a commitment to developing learners who are creative problem solvers. The words "creative problem solving" evoked smiles of satisfaction and were used throughout the following months as the school-community council drafted its proposal to the state board of education for restructuring the curriculum, instruction, and assessment.

During the opening session for school staff that next fall, the teachers met to begin developing curricular units, implementing hands-on and cooperative learning strategies, and selecting and creating assessments that would provide insights into student growth in each vision area. Thinking that "creative problem solving" was most closely related to the existing curriculum (as compared to something like "self-confident risk taking"), it was selected as the starting point. A classroom assessment specialist arrived to work with teachers and asked the question, "What does creative problem solving look like?" Thus began the multi-year effort to define the learning targets embedded in everyone's visionary goals.

In an early meeting, teachers agreed that this part of the vision was not limited to mathematics. They challenged each other to think broadly about the kinds of problems that children encounter throughout their day. Early brainstorming resulted in some of the following descriptors:

- Students can apply what they know in a new way.
- Students can state the problem as a question.
- Students can identify the key information in the problem.
- Students can plan a process for solving a problem.
- Students can carry out their plan successfully.
- Students can describe what they did and why.

While some uncertainties remained, it was time to try things out. Almost immediately there were additional concerns. Questions and issues about defining the target expanded:

- Is creative problem solving something new for the child?
- Is it something that involves applying what they know in a new way?
- What are "problems?" Is everything that kids learn for the first time a problem?
- Is it creative problem solving when the student comes up with a process or solution that is "new" for her but not necessarily unique? Does "creative" have to mean "unique?"
- Does every response to a problem have to be creative?
- Isn't it possible to have a solution that is elegant in its simplicity and efficiency but is not particularly creative?
- How can we help our students understand what we're aiming for?
- What is "creative" for very young learners?

A kindergarten teacher summed up her frustration: "It feels like I have to reshape the whole curriculum into problems—but I still don't know what we're looking for." And a fourth grade teacher said, "I don't want this to become a set of steps that students memorize; that misses the point." No one seemed able to find a way out of this dilemma. Everyone had labeled a target but couldn't define—let alone assess—it.

Initial Reflections

1. What are the sources of frustration in this case?
2. If you could talk with the teachers at this school, what questions would you ask?

3. What experiences do you have that can contribute to the discussion of this case?
4. How could you help others focus on the central issues?

Discussion Starters

1. How do we deal with something that is greatly valued but whose definition is vague?
2. What would you recommend to this group?
3. How might its members more fully define the target?
4. Should they revisit the school-community vision?
5. What assessment implications do you see as this group continues its work?

3.3 HOW DO WE BUILD COMMON MEANING? DEFINING HABITS OF MIND

A few months back, a classroom assessment specialist worked with a group of art educators in a school noted for its strong academic program and the independence afforded its teachers. The five high school teachers were very familiar with the use of performance assessments, especially products, portfolios, and exhibitions to document the growth of students' artistic skills and knowledge. Depending on the course, they required students to put together portfolios of their "best" work as final demonstrations of accomplishment, but these same teachers were struggling with the task of developing performance standards for the less tangible outcomes that they valued. As the discussion expanded, the phrase "habits of mind" struck a chord with the group. The phrase emerged as a useful description for qualities like persistence and risk taking, which help individuals be disposed to care passionately and use their artistic skills and knowledge thoughtfully.

The specialist working with this group was struck by the teachers' complete agreement that producing artists was not their chief purpose. In their individual areas, each felt that assessment based only on the quality of final products was inappropriate and would limit students' opportunities to make art a meaningful part of their lives.

The teachers' conversations revealed both the school culture and their group's deep commitment to fostering habits of mind and dispositions of the artist in their students. Whether the subject was pottery, graphic design, painting, architecture, or art history, these teachers sought to develop in students the desire to look at the world from a variety of perspectives and points of view. Gradually, other dimensions of the artist's dispositions began to take shape. They included persistence, risk taking, the ability to learn from unsuccessful work, and the ability to communicate about what they were learning.

The assessment specialist asked the group how such dispositions were assessed. Four members indicated that they "sensed" changing dispositions but weren't sure how to gather information formally. One talked of having students keep a log of sketches, reflections, notes, and project ideas. While delighted with the growing depth of her students' writing in these logs, she wasn't sure how to respond to them. Should she ask students to write about their developing habits of mind and dispositions? How would she know that they were not just writing what SHE wanted, rather than thoughtfully assessing their own growth? Her colleagues chimed in with ideas for posting the first draft of valued habits of mind, then having students talk about them and cite evidence that would back up their judgments. The discussion was flowing beautifully, and ideas for addressing habits of mind in other classes were generated. Here's the group's first draft of valued Habits of Mind and Dispositions:

THE ARTIST'S HABITS OF MIND[2]

Persistence

Problem Solving   *Risk Taking*

Craftsmanship   *Caring Passionately*

Collaboration   *Putting Together*
                                Seemingly Unrelated Things

Being Aware of the Choices You Make

Just before the bell rang signaling the end of their time with the assessment specialist and the return of students to class, one of the teachers looked up with dismay and said the single word *grades*. How would self-reported information about student dispositions ever fit into the requirements of cut off scores for grades? Would it be a separate reporting category? Would each disposition be reported separately? Would there be points for evidence of risk taking? What does persistence really look like? How would we know if a "failure" in one project contributed to success in another? How could we clearly describe each habit of mind so that communication about dispositions would be based on common definitions and examples?

As she ran out the door, the teacher who began the discussion said she was going to work on a scheme for incorporating the assessment of student dispositions into one of her current classes. She asked the others to think some more about the assessment issues and come prepared to make practical suggestions at their next department meeting.

Initial Reflections

1. Do the "habits of mind" identified by these teachers echo some of your own valued learning outcomes?
2. Are there others that are particularly important in your own situation?
3. Do you and your students have clear and shared meanings for such valued dispositions?
4. What strategies might you have used to build common understanding?

Discussion Starters

As one of the teachers in this department, contribute your ideas to the upcoming meeting:

1. Should the "habits of mind" identified by your department be included among the learning outcomes that are assessed? Why? Why not? If yes, how?
2. How can targets like "habits of mind" and "dispositions" be clearly and more fully defined?
3. What are possible barriers to quality assessment of "habits of mind"? Pathways that avoid the barriers?
4. Knowing that this school requires numeric grades of the teachers in this department, what would you advise?
5. How could you prompt students to provide honest and serious reporting of their developing dispositions?
6. What options other than student self-assessment might you use? How?

3.4 DEVELOPING MULTIPLE CRITERIA

A high school social studies meeting evolved into an interesting discussion. The objective of the meeting was to formulate plans for a new series of course final examinations mandated by the school board. In response to concerns that those teaching the same course might be setting different expectations, conducting different examinations, and assigning grades according to different standards, the board decided to require comparable exams in all like courses. Faculty members were meeting to begin implementing this requirement.

As they began to discuss their objectives it became clear that they did, in fact, expect different things of their students. Some emphasized student mastery of content knowledge. Others emphasized reasoning and problem-solving processes—that is, the ability to apply new knowledge.

As they discussed their uniform final exams, the teachers decided they would rely at least in part on essay questions. This would permit the assessment of both of the above-mentioned targets. Further, one teacher pointed out, their students sometimes had difficulty writing well enough to communicate what they had learned. That's why the English faculty had asked for the writing-across-the-curriculum program last year. So the social studies faculty should be evaluating writing skills, too. The essay format would help them do just that.

Another teacher protested that the use of essays would result in the need to evaluate each student's response to each essay exercise in terms of three different sets of scoring criteria. One would have to center on the student's success in demonstrating mastery of required content knowledge. The second would have to focus on the quality of student reasoning. And the third would have to reflect standards of writing proficiency. It is conceivable, this teacher pointed out, for a student to perform well on one out of three, two out of three, or all three of these facets of achievement.

"That's true," said yet another team member. "But think about it. It might be possible for us to devise a set of performance-rating criteria or checklists for each of these facets that would be generally applicable to whatever essay question we pose. If we succeeded in developing such generic criteria, once the students all learned to apply them, the scoring process would become very efficient."

The department chair reflected briefly and added, "And if our students could learn those criteria, our teaching job would become a whole lot easier, too. Not only would their achievement tasks become clear, there wouldn't be so much complaining among the students who fail to perform."

Initial Reflections

1. Assume that you are the social studies faculty. Take a first pass at outlining those three sets of performance standards. On what common basis might the faculty evaluate student mastery of content as represented in responses to different essay questions? Is this even feasible, or must scoring criteria be unique to each essay exercise?

2. On what common basis might the faculty evaluate reasoning proficiency? Can you outline what might be assessed across different essay exercises?

3. On what basis might they evaluate writing proficiency across exercises?

Discussion Starters

1. After you deliberate and collect your thoughts about these various standards of performance, is it the case that a student's proficiency might differ across them?

2. If so, which standard(s) should count in determining the student's social studies test grade?

3. If more than one should count, how might the criteria be differentially weighted in determining the grade on an essay test?

Notes

[1]Adapted from Martin Weirlangt, *Name the Graph* (Pohnpei State Department of Education, 1995). A work in progress. Reprinted by permission.
[2]Carol Jacovelli, *Habits of Mind* (Honolulu, 1995). A work in progress. Reprinted by permission.

4

Understanding All of the Assessment Alternatives

4.1 A DEBATE ABOUT APPROPRIATE WAYS OF ASSESSING

You have decided to attend a state-sponsored conference on assessment methods. Among the sessions you attend is a discussion of the relationship between assessment methods and achievement expectations. One presenter contends that the heavy dominance of multiple-choice tests in schools breeds a population of students and teachers that sees the world only in terms of right and wrong answers, though life rarely presents us with problems that are black or white. These tests, the speaker says, deliver the wrong message to students.

Another contributor chimes in with results of an action research study she did in her school in which she found that virtually 100 percent of the questions teachers asked of their students during instruction had one correct answer that the teacher was looking for. No questions asked for shades of gray or for student opinions. More evidence, she claims, of the impact of multiple-choice tests. She, too, urges abandonment of this way of assessing.

Yet another speaker reminds everyone that many cultures, including many European countries, have never "gone bonkers" over multiple-choice tests, and they seem to do fine, both in international assessments of achievement and in "real life." What, this person asks, is the big deal with multiple-choice tests anyway? Why do we not follow the lead of other countries?

The last contributor to the panel discussion provides several examples of multiple-choice test items that are obviously biased in favor of one group of students or another. Here, he contends, is the final piece of evidence that this testing format is fatally flawed and incapable of providing dependable information about student achievement.

All of these educators advocate the abandonment of the multiple-choice test format. All say if we wish assessments that set students up to function effectively in the real world, we should stick with performance assessments. Authentic assessment, they contend, delivers the right message.

Initial Reflections

1. Do you agree or disagree with their conclusion? Why?
2. Does real life present us with assessments that involve issues, questions, or decision-making circumstances that have right and wrong answers?
3. Should schools present students with questions that have right or wrong answers?
4. In school, does the answer to this question differ across different subject matter areas? If so, how?

Discussion Starters

1. Divide your group in half. Assign one half responsibility for defending selected-response assessment. The other half is to oppose its use. Strive to defend the point of view assigned. Then trade positions so you have to argue the other side. Which side is easier to defend and to refute? Why?
2. What implications does all of this have for the nature of our assessments—across different grades and disciplines? After all, some of our highest-stakes tests are collections of multiple-choice items.

4.2 THE DILEMMA OF DEFINING COMPLEX LEARNING

On an isolated island atoll in the Pacific Ocean, community elders, parents, traditional chiefs, and teachers are taking steps to build an assessment system tightly connected to their vision for the future. They began by "heart-storming"—digging deeply into their hopes and dreams for their children, their villages, and the islands that bind them together. Their initial heart-storming session led to the "Outcomes We Value" list that appears at the top of the facing page.

OUTCOMES WE VALUE[1]

Schooling should help students become:
Responsible citizens
Skillful adults
Self-reliant
Respectful, caring
Lifelong learners
Healthy
Wise decision makers and problem solvers
Knowledgeable about their own and other cultures

To expand and enrich their work, the assembled community then examined visions and values from other communities. From notes taken during a bilingual education meeting in rural Alaska, they selected and adapted descriptions that matched their own hopes and dreams[2]

- knowledge of language
- respect for others
- love for children
- knowledge of family
- respect for nature
- humor
- humility

- sharing
- respect for elders
- hard work
- avoidance of conflict
- spirituality
- family roles
- responsibility to the group

They also affirmed and adapted ideas from a vision for Pacific children developed by educational leaders:

> . . . *we envision a deep and abiding respect for self and others. . . .*
> *We wish for all our children to have the ability and commitment to*
> *maintain and sustain their culture(s) while valuing and being*
> *able to function in others. . . . We wish Pacific children to have a*
> *deep sense of responsibility for the society in which they live; to*
> *care for the environment, placing a priority on preserving and*
> *protecting it. We wish our children to live in a world in which peo-*
> *ple are valued for their uniqueness as well as the things they have*
> *in common. We wish this so our children and our children's chil-*
> *dren will have the capacity to cherish the past while being pre-*
> *pared for the future.*[3]

While the vision was growing in its detail and the community and school were moving toward shared understanding, there was uncertainty about the next step. Does the vision go anywhere from here? How can and should it affect our actions? In school? In the family? In the community?

As part of a long-term assessment project, trainers from the capital island and their coaches came to do a series of school visits. Arriving on a small plane, the group was met by the regional high school principal who had requested a vision-assessment session for her teachers before the trainers departed by boat for follow-up school visits the next day.

In order to help teachers look closely at the vision-assessment connections that already exist, determine those that ought to be developed, and identify actions that were needed, the high school session began with small groups adding descriptions to each component of the vision. Together, group members began to develop a matrix and to look for curriculum connections. The group chose to begin with "self-sufficiency," and the chalk board began to fill up with ideas in response to several key questions:

1. What kinds of learning targets are part of achieving the vision?

2. Looking at each target separately, is each currently being assessed? Directly? Indirectly? Not at all?

3. What forms of assessment are being used to provide information about the targets?

4. How confident are we about the quality of the information we are currently getting about the targets (on a scale from 1-5, with 1 being no confidence and 5 being a high degree of confidence)?

5. Do we need to use additional or different forms of assessment to get accurate and clear pictures of learning related to targets? Which forms are useful for these types of targets?

6. What action steps do we need to take to move from where we are now toward quality assessment information?

As the work continued, small groups began to discuss the role of the schools in fostering self-sufficiency and the degree to which the existing curriculum, current ways of teaching, and the assessment honored the traditional ways of learning in the home.

One teacher spoke of the separate lives she leads at school and in the family and community:

> So much of learning in our culture comes through observation over time with little direct instruction—questions and answer patterns between teachers and student. It is the role of children to absorb what they see and hear; to learn in informal ways in a place where they are around people of many different ages. I've spent time in courses and had in-service on lots of strategies; but I still wonder if we're really losing one part of ourselves in order to gain a new self. Sometimes when my students are struggling, I know the strategies aren't working for them. I've wondered at times if they were just too far behind, but when I watch them doing things at home, they are skillful, careful, and make choices thoughtfully. When I test them in school, they can't show what they know. It seems as though this might be our chance to use some other ways

of assessment to let us see into their school learning. Do some of these other forms of assessment match our ways of knowing and show learning better?

One elder, who took little visible part in the early discussion, spoke:

We've felt that the schools were separate from our lives—from the family and the culture—that learning our ways of knowing and doing culture was the responsibility of the family, and learning things from outside was the responsibility of the school and the teachers. Yet as we look at our teenagers' grades, as well as their actions in the community, we have begun to worry that our young people are losing in both school and culture. For a self-sufficient future we must deal with the continuation of who we are as a people and what we need to know to thrive elsewhere. If schools can help, it's time to work together. Some of the knowledge that has been held in the culture needs to be shared.

A young man, recently returned home from post-secondary schooling outside the community, tentatively expressed his thoughts:

As I look at the things we've written so far, none of them are things that can only be learned in the family. They are things that are joint responsibility. The coaches have told us that what we assess communicates what we value. Then we must expand our assessments to include things valued at home as well as abroad. To do that, we have to use more than tests. It's not just in our culture that there are important learnings that don't fit a particular type of assessment. People in many other places are looking at designing assessment systems that enable the whole school and its community to get rich, detailed, and accurate pictures of learning.

Initial Reflections

1. Reflect on and write your own definition of self-sufficiency or another component of your personal vision for the future of the young people you work with. While the setting and culture of the community in the above case might be unlike your own, are common concerns and issues being raised?

2. Do you recall students whose ways of knowing and showing their learning differed significantly from their peers?

Discussion Starters

1. Does your community discuss the role of schooling as the community in the this case did? Should communities do so? Why?

2. What does it mean to be self-sufficient in your culture? Is this an important achievement target?

3. Is it possible to align key elements of a target like self-sufficiency to appropriate assessment methods?

4. Do you think it's a good idea to offer students a choice of assessment modes to demonstrate what they know and can do? Why or why not?

5. How should self-sufficiency be assessed? With one method? Many? Which one(s)?

6. Should assessment be the same for all students?

4.3 THE CASE OF THE RESTRICTIVE POLICY

Assume that this article appears in your newspaper describing events in your school district:

> Teachers in this community have worked hard over the years to develop standards for judging student work, without having a formal district evaluation policy.
>
> Although administrators agree that a grading policy is needed, the policy presented by the school board has met harsh criticism. In a district known for quality students and top notch academic programs, the proposed assessment and grading policy has frustrated some parents. The proposed policy excludes group projects, student performances, and portfolios, calling for total reliance solely on "traditional" assessments such as tests and essays.
>
> The plan holds that "performance-based assessment and portfolios are considered inappropriate . . . and will not be used" and that most classroom time should be devoted to "the acquisition of knowledge not student demonstrations . . . or amassing collections of student work."
>
> The ban on performance-based assessments raises questions from several parents who believe such assessments are a natural part of life.
>
> "This policy puts us back decades," said one. "What about the student who's not a good test taker? Is that student less valuable because he can't take a test well? Does that mean there's no other way to show what's been learned?"

"In real life, interpersonal skills and group work are used every day, and when we don't reflect that in the classroom, we short change the kids," said another. "I haven't taken a multiple choice test on the job lately, but the test of my abilities happens every time I get together with someone and we can accomplish something."

Both the administration and one school board member agree that different forms of assessment complement the learning process, and it's "illogical" to think one method has to be sacrificed for another.

So far, only that board member has voiced strong opposition to the proposed policy as written. He points out that the administration has not yet fully explained to the board how performance-based assessments have been used in the past and how they can contribute in the future.

The superintendent agrees. "Now it's a matter of going back and reviewing this policy, because if it's approved as is, it will disable teachers and many of our practices will be in jeopardy," he said. He added that he expects revisions to be made before the policy is approved.

Initial Reflections

1. What do you think is motivating the school board?
2. What knowledge base, if any, is the board missing?
3. What is your reaction to the superintendent's role in this situation?

Discussion Starters

1. Is this a sound policy? Why?
2. Your job is to do the presentation that reveals to the board the implications of its policy. What would you do to prepare for that presentation? What would you include in your presentation?
3. How can the community's concerns about this policy be addressed?
4. What role should the superintendent play in addressing this controversy?

Notes

[1]Developed as part of the Yap Classroom Learning Assessment, Yap Department of Education, 1993.

[2]From *Inupiaq Values*. Adapted from a presentation by Rachel Craig, Alaska Bilingual-Bicultural Education Conference, Anchorage, 1983.
[3]Adapted from *Our Vision of the Pacific Child* (Honolulu: Pacific Regional Educational Laboratory, 1990).

5

Facing the Barriers to Quality Assessment

5.1 WHEN CAN I GO TO THE BATHROOM? THE BARRIER OF TIME

This case returns us to the student-centered school found in Chapter 2, Case 2.1, The Dilemma of Differing Assessment Purposes, and Chapter 3, Case 3.2, What in the World Is Creative Problem Solving? The context for this case will be clearer as you take a look back at your notes and reflections.

To demonstrate that the assessment system currently under development can provide school-level information, teachers at a student-centered elementary school agreed to conduct and summarize reading interviews. They sampled students across grade levels and used the initial results to polish and refine their interview questions. Students were selected to represent a spread of performance, and teachers began to schedule the interviews.

One section of the interview focuses on student's ability to "construct meaning." These were the questions asked:[1]

- Tell me about the book you have selected for this conference.
- Why do you think the author wrote this book?
- Would you recommend this book? Why or why not?

Additional sections of the interview protocol invite students to demonstrate wide reading through their book lists, silent/oral reading, and use of reading strategies, attitudes toward reading, and self-assessment. The final section of the interview sheet provides space for notes about next steps and adjustments to instruction.

After their initial interviews, teachers met to discuss their experiences. One said, "I don't know how anyone can do these new assessments and still have time to teach. I only had five students to interview, but it took me more than 90 minutes to do the first one. If I hadn't had a student teacher in my room, I couldn't have done it."

Another teacher chimed in: "I really learned a lot about my students when we got going on the interviews, and I'd like to do this with all of them. But I started to wonder, how could I ever find the time to conduct interviews with 28 students?"

A third grade teacher who had conducted interviews earlier in the year to probe students' problem solving commented: "This reading assessment was different. At least they had a book to talk about. When I tried to interview a few of my students about their everyday problem solving, it took more than a half hour of prompting on my part for a student even to remember the details of the unit, and I found myself telling them things about the activities to help them remember. The completed interviews took more than 90 minutes each. These reading interviews were a little shorter, but still, how do I keep all of my students going while I'm doing interviews?"

Someone suggested using parent volunteers or university college of education "observation" students to conduct the interviews. The third grade teacher replied, "But I'm the one who needs to get the insights into my individual students so I can adjust my teaching. If I let someone else do the interviews, they might not look for or see the things that will trigger action on my part. They just don't know my students the way I do. I thought that was one of the main reasons for our using multiple forms of assessment—to gain really useful and complex portraits of our students' learning so we can make good instructional decisions."

As their reflection session came to an end, "When will I ever have time to go to the bathroom?" was the comic but very real parting question.

Initial Reflections

1. Obviously, time is the issue here. Why has it emerged so strongly in this case? Be specific. What's going wrong?

Discussion Starters

1. How would you advise this group? Should everyone continue using the reading interview? Why?

2. What are some practical ways of dealing with the time issue?

3. Are there other assessment alternatives? What are the pluses and minuses of each?

5.2 CHICKENS AND PIGS: LANGUAGE THAT INHIBITS ASSESSMENT[2]

An assessment workshop presenter tells a story of a training experience in a Pacific island culture:

"I'd chosen an activity that I had had great success with in the past. It had never failed to engage teachers in lively discussion and prompt thinking beyond the 'correct' answer. One of my purposes was to help teachers clarify what they value in student problem solving—and then to build preliminary criteria from the key qualities of excellent work identified in their small-group discussions. Here's what the task looked like that morning:

Problem: Ignacia and Cal went outside to feed the animals. They saw both chickens and pigs. Cal said: "I see 18 animals in all." Ignacia answered: "Yes, and altogether they have 52 legs." How many chickens and how many pigs were in the yard?

"I had found the original task in several sources. The task seemed appropriate because the mathematics involved chickens and pigs, both found in outer islands. I had eliminated the beginning of the task that placed the children in a barnyard, because there are no barns and no farms in outer island communities. Thinking to make the task even more appropriate for the island context, I changed the names of the two children in the task to ones found in this culture.

"Teachers began examining the task and some sample student responses. Discussing the task in their own language, they turned puzzled faces toward me. Finally, a senior member of the group asked if I realized that in their language there was one word for 'limbs' and it refers to both the wings and feet of a chicken! A lively discussion ensued about possible hidden factors that could mask student's capabilities and understanding.

"With a smile, another teacher pointed out that the children in the task wouldn't need to ponder the problem, they'd just look at the animals and count each kind. (It was a quick lesson in authenticity for me!) I was suddenly much more deeply aware of the complexity of getting clear and accurate pictures of learning across cultures and languages.

"I had a similar experience in a midwestern school. This time it was not language that blocked quality assessment, but the context and experience of the learners.

"On a statewide assessment, children were given a selected-response item that asked them to identify the number of legs on a chicken. Children from rural communities had no trouble providing the expected answer—2. City children, whose experience of chickens rested solely on those found in frozen packages in the grocery store, responded 4. When questioned, the children said that all the chickens they'd seen had four legs showing in the package.

"I worry still about how to overcome this kind of barrier. A question that I've begun to share each time I work with a group is this: *How can our assessments promote excellence in each student? Demand real intellectual quality* <u>*while*</u> *honoring their culture(s)? Their environment(s)? Their ways of knowing and showing their learning?* What do you think?

Initial Reflections

1. Is there a story from your own experience in which a quality assessment issue was hidden or difficult to recognize?

2. In preparation for your case discussion, select an assessment task or item that presents potential problems for students whose language and culture are not the same as that of the developers. Underline parts of the task that could be changed to improve it.

Discussion Starters

1. Examine the sample items and tasks your group has assembled. What are some ways in which the tasks could pose problems for children of diverse cultures? Children whose first language is not English?

2. How might each item or task be repaired to help gain a clearer picture of the learning target?

3. What are some assessment formats that do not require, or that minimize, written language requirements? What are the advantages and disadvantages of each in terms of creating a clear picture of learning?

5.3 "THIS TOO SHALL PASS." THE TEACHER WHO IS SET IN HIS WAYS

The staff meeting began 15 minutes late as usual—what with the gathering of busy faculty and the time allowed for refreshments. Just a few minutes to talk with colleagues is a small but important luxury, especially after a long summer apart. Everyone at the high school has so much to catch up on.

Finally, the principal begins with the usual kinds of notes and directives from the district office covering the issues addressed at the school board meeting a few days ago: bus transportation, the upcoming bond issue, the need to adjust to smaller budgets.

Then the meeting turns to the topic of priorities in the district's strategic plan. This year, topic number one is assessment. A district-wide committee has been appointed by the superintendent to review assessment procedures and recommend changes to the school board. Because assessment reforms seem to be sweeping the nation, this district needs to find out what's going on and get on the band wagon. The principal doesn't seem to have a clear sense of what to do or to expect here, so she simply asks that the faculty participate in whatever planning, assessment, or professional development activities come up.

A social studies teacher in the back of the room asks, "Why does the superintendent think anything needs to change from an assessment perspective? It seems as though everything has been going pretty well. We had two national merit scholars last year. We have more kids taking advanced placement exams in history than ever before, and they're scoring very well. Average college admissions test scores are higher than ever. If I were in charge, I don't think I would want to change anything. I don't want people looking over my shoulder when I assess. We don't need any strategic plan priority on assessment."

A colleague from the math department chimes in, "Yeah, but what percent of our graduates go on to college—about 40 percent. And that's great, but what about the rest? How are they doing? I was collared the other day by the owner of a local restaurant who knows I'm a math teacher. She asked if we ever taught the kids anything out at that brand new $25 million high school. 'Sure,' I said, 'why?' She showed me an example of some simple math one of our recent graduates screwed up. Then she laughed and told me there had been some frustrated talk about this at Rotary last week. I checked and this kid graduated with a GPA of 2.85, 45th in a class of 195—not too bad!"

Back to the social studies teacher, "Look, my students are succeeding. I had a letter just the other day from an old friend who's a professor at the university telling me how pleased she was with one of our graduates. If your students are failing the test of real life, you deal with it. Don't ask me to take responsibility for it or to change everything. I'm doing the job I was hired to do."

At this point the principal steps in: "We've got conflicting impressions, both here at school and in the community. It seems as though the assessment picture isn't really clear within the school. We need to check the accuracy of the perceptions about our students' performance and then make some decisions. One of the reasons the superintendent wants us to look more closely at assessment is facing us right now. What solid evidence do we have about student learning? How does it jibe with the conflicting impressions we've heard? Are both perspectives accurate? Is there a difference in performance by subject? If so, we need to consider how we'll communicate to the whole community what our students' strengths and needs are and what actions we're going to take to address the needs. We have to think in terms of solid evidence and help the community view student performance in the same way."

One teacher suggests that it might be useful to conduct a community survey of graduates. Another recommends surveying local businesses. But the teacher who opened up the discussion by citing how well his students were doing is still adamant: "My kids are doing fine. I teach Social Studies and I'm tough. If students don't want to work hard in my class, then they don't sign up for my electives. If there are problems in the math department, leave me out of it."

Each teacher cites different evidence of the effectiveness of his or her teaching. Their views of the school's public relations differ fundamentally. One teacher sees very positive regard from the community, while another sees just the opposite—a public relations nightmare in the making. Both are citing compelling assessment evidence that they're right.

Initial Reflections

1. Analyze the evidence being presented on both sides. From the perspective of sound assessment (i.e., applying our five standards of assessment quality), do you see any reason for concern about that quality on either side? Identify the basis of your concerns, if any.

2. Is it possible that both are right? Wrong? How could this be?

Discussion Starters

The principal has requested your assistance for the next meeting of her staff when the above discussion will continue. In preparation, she asked you to think about these questions:

1. What evidence is there of student learning? How solid and accurate do you think it is?

2. How can this school check to see whose impression is correct? What kinds of assessment could be used to build a schoolwide profile of learning?

3. If there's a survey of recent graduates, what questions should be asked? How should it be designed?

4. If there's a survey of businesses and the community, what questions should be asked? How should the survey be designed?

5. How would you approach the first teacher to involve him or her more directly in the process?

Notes

[1]Adapted by Waialae Elementary School from the Upper Arlington Holistic Reading Assessment, 1995.

[2]Adapted from *Chickens and Pigs: A Toolkit for Professional Developers* (Alternative Assessment, Laboratory Network Program, Northwest Regional Educational Laboratory, Portland, Oregon, 1994).

6

Selected-Response
Assessment

6.1 THE DILEMMA OF MULTIPLE-CHOICE TEST BIAS

You teach in a large urban high school in an ethnically mixed neighborhood. In order to maintain high standards of academic rigor, your faculty voted to institute common final examinations in courses taught by different teachers. To make this work, teachers meet within departments to compare knowledge and reasoning targets, devise tables of test specifications, write test items, and assemble multiple-choice tests. They consider using essay exercises, performance assessments, and personal-communication assessments where appropriate, but due to the time constraints of the faculty, few of these are developed.

To help deal with the time crunch, the district is providing centralized optical scanner test-scoring services for the faculty. (The district even bought the newest scanner technology for this purpose.) The software package includes test-analysis capabilities that stretch far beyond the teachers' understanding and needs.

Several days after the finals have been administered and scored and grades have been assigned, you receive an urgent message from the principal to come immediately to a meeting in the office. Upon arriving, you find a small committee of parents representing various ethnic communities. They have in hand a computer printout listing final exam scores by student, with students listed in ethnic groups. These scores reflect student performance on the final exam developed by your department. At the end of each section of the list is an average score for all students in that ethnic category. Southeast

Asian students have the highest average, followed by Caucasian students. On average, Black and Hispanic students scored considerably lower.

The parents are contending that these differences in average performance represent compelling evidence that the test is biased against a student's ethnic heritage and should be discarded. Based on the facts presented, are they correct in this assertion?

Initial Reflections

1. As you work through this dilemma, think about what it means for a test to be biased in favor of or against someone. Is evidence of different levels of performance on the test compelling evidence that it is biased against the low scorers?
2. Also remember to consider the attributes of a quality assessment. What role might they play in working through this dilemma? Remember particularly the various sources of bias and distortion. What might have gone wrong here? Might any sources have been overlooked?

Discussion Starters

1. What action should be taken here? What should the principal do next? The teachers? The community representatives? Who has what responsibilities in this case?
2. How should the analysis of the test and student performance proceed? Brainstorm a set of appropriate actions and place them in the order in which you think work should be done.

6.2 THE CHALLENGE OF FIXING A TROUBLED TEST

Your fifth grade science textbook comes with a packet of already developed unit tests. One unit guides students through the development of a fish tank. The brief instructional unit and the associated multiple-choice test (with table of specifications) follow. Is this a good test or not? If you find flaws, please fix them.

INSTRUCTIONAL UNIT[1]
SETTING UP A TROPICAL FISH TANK

Have you ever thought of setting up a fish tank as a hobby? It's fun and easy to do. To get started, you need seven things: a tank, some gravel, a pump, an underwater filter, a light, a heater, and water. Of course, you also need a place to put the tank and a place to plug in the heater, pump, and light. That's it. You don't need fish. They come later. Don't be in a hurry to put fish into a new tank. If you rush things, you'll kill them.

Don't buy any tank smaller than 20 gallons. Bigger is better. A 10-gallon tank will only hold a very few very small fish. Figure out where you want the tank before you set it up; it's tough to move later. You don't have to buy a special stand, but make sure that whatever you set the tank on will hold plenty of weight. A 20-gallon tank filled with water weighs well over 150 pounds. Put the tank somewhere away from light. Even small amounts of natural light encourage the growth of algae which, though actually beneficial to some fish, will also cloud the water and turn it an unattractive murky green.

When you have your tank where you want it, install the filter. This needs to go in before anything else. Do not plug anything in yet, however. Next add the gravel. You need 10 pounds for every 10 gallons of water in the tank. You don't need to rinse or clean gravel from a pet store; it's ready to go.

Once the gravel is in place, add the water. Use clear water from your tap. It's a good idea to add dechlorinator to neutralize any chemicals in the water before adding fish. Dechlorinator is available from any pet shop. Fill the tank close to the top, remembering that you will need to add the heater.

Next, hook up the heater. Set it to 80 degrees. Make sure it's well submerged in the tank. Most heaters are fully submersible, cord and all. Be careful not to set the temperature too high; not all fish can tolerate water temperatures approaching 90 degrees or more.

Finally turn on the light, admire how nice everything looks, and plug in the pump to activate your filter system. Keep in mind that the pump forces air through the system. As you turn it up, you add more air to the water. You also move the water around more. Some species of fish do well with all that commotion but others do not, so keep this in mind later when you choose your fish.

Finally, let the tank "cure" for five to ten days—or even more, if you can stand the wait. This allows for establishment of healthful bacteria to deal with pollution in the tank. When you're finally ready to add the fish, add just a <u>few</u>—perhaps one (or two at most) for every five gallons until you are sure the bacteria are sufficiently well established to keep your fish alive.

Next unit: "Choosing Fish for the New Tank."

TEST SPECIFICATION CHART

| Chapter Subject: | Freshwater Fish Tanks |
| Grade: | Grades 5-8 |

Content	Recall	Analysis	Inference	Evaluation
Setting up the new tank	4	2	6	1

UNIT TEST

Multiple Choice

1. About how much gravel do you need for a new tank?
   a.   About 10 pounds.
   b.* About 10 pounds for every 10 gallons of water.
   c.   It depends on the size of the tank.
   d.   About 1,000 pounds.

2. Of the seven basic items you need to start up a new fish tank, which of the following is not one of them?
   a.* Fish.
   b.   Gravel.
   c.   A filter.
   d.   All of the above.

3. The first step in setting up a new fish tank is to:
   a.   buy a fish.
   b.   buy the tank.
   c.* put the tank where you want it.
   d.   put in the water.

4. The main purpose of dechlorinator is to:
   a.   to kill algae in the water.
   b.   encourages the growth of beneficial bacteria.
   c.   it cleans the gravel.
   d.* make the water safe for fish.

5. If you add fish to a new tank too soon, which of the following undesirable results will occur?
   a.   The fish will get sick.
   b.* The fish will die.
   c.   The fish will grow rapidly.
   d.   Healthful bacteria will begin to grow.

6. The main purpose of the air pump is to
   a.* pump air into the water.
   b.   empty water from the tank.

    c.   keep the fish moving at a fast pace.

    d.   stir up the water so it will look cloudy.

7. It would probably be a good idea to set up a new fish tank:

    a.   near a window.

    b.   on a small bookcase.

    c.   slowly, taking your time.

    d.* close to an electrical outlet.

True-False

8. It is a good idea to not put a new fish tank too far away from natural light.

    True   False

9. Natural light can stimulate the growth of algae, thus killing some fish.

    True   False

Fill-in

10. You should set the temperature in your tank at _____ .

11. After your fish tank has cured for _____ weeks, add _____ fish for every _____ gallons of _____ .

Matching

12. Match items on the left with those on the right. Use each item on the right once or more than once.

a. Pump _____	1. Cleans the water.
b. Filter _____	2. Reduces pollution.
c. Algae _____	3. Adds air to water.
d. Heater _____	4. Dangerous to fish.
e. Bacteria _____	5. Turns water murky.
f. Filter _____	6. Harmful to fish.
g. Fish _____	7. Create commotion in the tank.
h. Dechlorinator _____	8. 90 degrees
i. Pollution _____	9. 80 degrees
j. Light _____	10. Don't add too soon.
k. Gravel _____	11. Helpful to fish.
	12. Kills fish.
	13. Add last.
	14. Add first.
	15. Causes algae.
	16. Ready to go.
	17. Helps show off fish attractively.

Essay

13. Choose one of the following and write a one-paragraph answer. (30 minutes, 50 points)

    a. It is important not to add new fish to your tank too soon. Explain why.

    b. Do you agree or disagree that setting up a new fish tank is a simple process? Explain your reasons.

Discussion Starters

1. When you have finished your analysis, compare your revisions with those of another participant. Do you agree?

6.3 MATCHING EXERCISES AND THINKING ACROSS LANGUAGES

During a workshop that introduced a group of high school teachers to guidelines for developing and improving selected-response items, there were opportunities for teachers to analyze various formats and make revisions based on guidelines that I (Kathy) had used successfully with many groups. Early in the workshop one of the English teachers reminded me that this is a school where most students are English Language Learners (ELL)—where the language of their home and, in this instance the community as well, is not the language of schooling. This situation poses some additional design considerations for teachers.

We reviewed guidelines for matching items and I set up small groups with the task of repairing some sample matching exercises. As I monitored each group's work, I was pleased to see guidelines coming to life in improved exercises. Each of the revised exercises contained 10 or fewer questions; the items were all of the same type—all events, all historical figures, all chemical formulas, all characters in the same story; and the questions and answer choices were now all at the same level of specificity. Finally, each set had more answers than questions. I was elated at the success of their work.

Then during presentations of each group's work, a question was posed that stumped me: If the guideline to keep the total number of questions to 10 or less is based on research about how much we can hold in our heads at the same time, should there be a smaller number for students who have to operate across languages?

I turned back to the group, whose experience with assessment across cultures was far greater than my own, and asked them what they thought about this question and what other questions they'd had as we progressed through the workshop. This opened up a floodgate of concerns these caring teachers had about their students, their language skills, and assessment.

An English teacher told the story of her eighth grade students, most of whom she was certain knew the social studies content of the test she had prepared. She said that things fell apart when they got to the matching section of the test. Was it the number of items? Did they need to have short words first (on the left side of the page) and lengthier answer choices on the right? She conjectured that students might be giving up when confronted with long phrases and sentences.

One teacher talked about using selected-response tests almost exclusively because her students' writing skills in their second or even third language were limited. She wanted to find ways to unlock the learning of her students and wondered how to enrich selected-response assessments. Several others wanted to learn how to make selected responses and short-answer questions that could tap into student's thinking and decision making. Another teacher was pessimistic. He felt that even though this type of assessment placed limited demands on students' writing skills, reading across languages presented a whole new set of challenges to ELL students.

We returned to a list of assessment principles from the opening of the workshop. One of the principles dealt directly with the issue at hand: The language of assessment must match the language of instruction. If not, assessment produces unfair and invalid results. Children must be fluent in the language in which they are to be assessed and the level of language must match their stage of development. This way of thinking was deemed appropriate by a group of educators who daily face children in classrooms where textbooks are in English, much of the instruction switches back and forth between English and the home language, and life decisions like entrance into high school depend on the students' test scores in English.

Initial Reflections

1. Assessment requires the sharing of information between teacher and student. Most assessment formats use language, spoken or written, to accomplish the exchange. Are there ways of sharing that are not language based?

2. When language-based assessment is used, how can teachers maximize the quality of communication? One way is to be sure they use the same language as their students. Are there others?

Discussion Starters

1. Do problems associated with the language of communication play out differently across one of four basic assessment methods? Can selected-response formats work with limited English language learners?

2. Should teachers accommodate language differences among their students? If so, how?

3. How can teachers verify the accuracy of their assessments with multicultural students?

6.4 FOCUSING ON IMPORTANT LEARNING: WHAT'S WORTH ASSESSING?

An assessment study group of middle school social studies teachers drafted selected-response test items in multiple-choice, true/false, matching, and short-answer formats. Design teams of teachers, principals, and specialists posted their work and then began a critical friends' review and critique. Each team reviewed the work of the others, writing commendations and suggestions for improvement, noting where guidelines were violated, and posing questions for the authors.

One set of items was developed around Pacific island government symbolic seals. Each seal contains images of the island state, its environment, cultural values, people, history, and unique features. Colors and design elements add meaning to each. The task for design teams was to use the seals, what they had learned about each island state in social studies classes, and their knowledge of symbols in their own homeland to develop a set of selected-response items—adhering to general guidelines for sound questions and the specific guidelines for each format.

First and second drafts were posted to enable reviewers to note improvements. The multiple-choice team was proud of its work, pleased that the list of commendations next to its questions grew longer as the review continued. There is a sampling at the top of the facing page:[2]

At first the groups were tentative in making comments and suggestions about their peers' work, but gradually the experience of cross-checking the items with guidelines for quality paper and pencil items led to some excellent suggestions. A few groups urged their colleagues to seek ways to make the items more challenging.

Toward the end of the critique session, one design team stood before the multiple-choice drafts shown above; they had completed their discussion. While the group felt that guidelines for designing sound multiple-choice items were followed, one of the teachers quietly raised a different concern. Pointing to Question 1 (How many items are there in our national seal?), he asked, "Is this worth assessing? It doesn't seem important enough to be worth testing. Maybe importance should be one of our criteria."

Another teacher argued that knowing the symbols and their meaning was really important, while a third suggested that one of the symbols, a star with 24 points, was important because the four largest points represent each of the regional centers and the other points indicate how many atolls (chains

---

1. How many items are there in our national seal?
   a. two items
   b. four items
   c. five items
   d. three items

2. What are the colors in our flag?
   a. Orange, white and yellow
   b. Orange, white and blue
   c. Red, yellow and white
   d. Red, blue and yellow

3. How many points are there on the star in our flag?
   a. 24
   b. 26
   c. 28
   d. 30

---

of low sandy islands) are part of the nation. The first teacher responded with another question: "Is it important to know how many points there are or to know what each point represents? What do we want our children to know about the symbols on our flag? What's worth knowing? What's the role of symbols in our sense of nationhood?"

Initial Reflections

1. Are there curriculum questions that need to be raised before the review and critique is completed? If so, what are they?

2. How might the items be enriched?

3. Can you think of an instance—as a student, parent, or teacher—when you took a test that included items you felt weren't worth learning or assessing? How did you react?

4. Are there any items that aren't worth assessing? Why?

Discussion Starters

1. What advice would you give as a member of the "critical friends" review team? How would you change the sample items?

2. In your own situation, how are decisions made about what's worth learning, teaching and assessing? Who has a say? In what ways are students involved?

3. With a partner, examine a selected-response assessment you've used recently. Is importance one of the criteria used to decide on the knowledge targets?

Notes

[1]From *Paper and Pencil Test Design.* A video training package (Portland, Oregon: Northwest Regional Educational Laboratory). Reprinted by permission.
[2]Adapted from RMI Assessment Coaches Training, 1996.

7

Essay Assessment:
Vast Untapped Potential

7.1 THE CASE OF THE SURPRISING ESSAY ASSESSMENT

The development of student writing proficiency has become a high priority in the school district where you have just been hired. In fact, in the brief orientation to your new teaching assignment you've come to see that "writing across the curriculum" has become the watchword. Everyone is to help students develop higher levels of writing proficiency.

In an attempt to do your part and to plan good "continuous progress" instruction, you decide to conduct a pre-assessment of your students' mastery of the material you intend to cover and you decide to do this using an essay assessment. You have set both knowledge and reasoning targets that the essay format fits well. On the second day of the new school year, you administer your assessment.

The results will give you a baseline from which to measure student gain over the course of the semester. The greater the gain, the higher the student's grade. You plan to be very systematic this time. No more hassles about the grades assigned in this school. Everyone will know the grading rules right from the start.

Your new job is very demanding—a badly overcrowded middle school where you face six classes per day totaling 196 students. You use essay pre-assessment in just two of your classes—for 66 students. But scoring won't be a problem, because you have your teacher's aid and a student teacher to help you read and evaluate student responses.

After school, the three of you are reading the student responses, assigning scores, entering the scores in the grade book, and discussing student performance. As an overall pattern of results begins emerge, you begin to draw conclusions about the strengths and weaknesses of your students so you can plan instruction accordingly. It's going just fine. Then—

Problem #1: All of a sudden, the student teacher looks up, groans, and utters the lament, "Oh my gosh, you're not going to believe this one." Upon checking, you see a test paper containing responses written totally in Spanish. None of you can read or speak Spanish.

Initial Reflections

1. What do you do next? What is the central issue here?
2. Is there compelling evidence in this test paper of a lack of achievement? How do you find out?

Discussion Starters

1. What are the implications of this situation for your achievement standards, teaching strategies, assessment strategies, and—most of all—your grading plan? What if this student can't write in English?
2. Is it fair to impose an "English Only" standard on students in terms of the attributes of a quality assessment?

Problem #2: A bit later in the scoring session, you come across a student paper that has the same response to every essay exercise: "I don't know the answer." No attempt is made to answer. But at the end of the paper you find a brief note from the student: "I really plan to gain a lot in this course—so I can get an A!"

Initial Reflections

1. Might the student seek to mislead you about beginning achievement? Why?
2. Does this incident raise any fairness questions (questions of equal opportunity for all students) about the procedures you plan to use to assign grades?

Discussion Starters

1. How do you deal with this paper? What are its implications for your assessment plans and plans to grade on improvement?

2. As you begin to keep your records of student achievement for grading purposes, what record do you enter into your system as the starting point for these two students?

7.2 WHAT DOES QUALITY LOOK LIKE? THE DILEMMA OF CONFLICTING COMMUNICATION PATTERNS

A Hawaii secondary social studies teacher was stuck. Teaching in a large high school with a multi-ethnic student body, she faced students with a wide variety of cultural and linguistic backgrounds, communication and self-presentation styles, and experience in written English. How was she going to be fair and set clear standards for all? Questions about interpreting the quality of student work across cultures were in the forefront of her mind. As this teacher began to examine responses to a recent essay assignment, she saw a familiar pattern emerging in the writing of some of her students from one particular Micronesian culture.

In their essays these students included key ideas but almost never elaborated on them or backed them up with additional details. There simply wasn't enough content in their writing to allow the teacher to make confident judgments about their mastery of key ideas and content. She felt that she was missing some pieces of a complex puzzle.

In class discussions, these students tended to offer brief comments only when prompted and were very uncomfortable when called on in front of the group. They often seemed to have caught the gist of the idea or concept but didn't go beyond simple statements. When called on in class, most would begin by apologizing for not knowing as much as their classmates. The teacher was leery of making generalizations about students from any culture, but she felt that here there was a clear pattern.

To help her analyze the situation, she sought out an educator from that culture. She wanted to get some answers that would help her understand her students' learning. "At first I thought it was primarily a language problem. I felt that the students had little experience writing in English and that I needed to encourage them to try out their ideas in writing—without focusing very much on form or conventions. I expected that after a while, their written language skills would improve to the point that I could look at their work with the same criteria I used for all of my other students. But even though I've seen improvements in their word choices, spelling, and punctuation, the writing still remains very minimal."

"What's going on? How can I get them to elaborate? I think it's really important for my students to reason well on paper and to back up the judgments they make. That's one of the reasons I'm using essay questions. I'm just not getting enough to know if that's happening."

Her friend helped clarify the issue. "In many Micronesian cultures, communicating clearly with the fewest words possible is a sign of knowledge and power. Someone who 'gets it' quickly and without elaboration shows deep understanding. When you're the one communicating, if you add lots of details, context, and examples, you're telling your listeners or readers that they can't 'get it' without all that extra help. Our cultures tend to be 'high context.' Most of the essential meaning is embedded in physical and non-verbal communication. American culture, by contrast, tends to value communication in which meaning is made more and more explicit through detailed verbal or written elaboration. There's a conflict for students here between the kinds of communication that are valued in their culture and the communication expectations they face in school."

Although the explanation provided useful insights into some reasons for the kinds of essays the teacher was receiving, she is still facing the dilemma of assessing the social studies knowledge and reasoning of her Micronesian pupils. Writing in their first language is not an option for many of her students. In their home islands, writing instruction stopped for most at the end of third grade.

Initial Reflections

1. What assessment problems does this case present?
2. Is quality assessment possible here?

Discussion Starters

1. Should this teacher expect and encourage her Micronesian students to provide more and more elaboration in their writing? Is it essential for their success that she do so? Why and how, or why not?
2. What specific strategies might be used to prompt students to elaborate?
3. Is it possible that the definition of excellent writing the teacher is currently using is too narrow? Are there different "faces of excellence" here?
4. Can you suggest some other assessment options and describe how each might contribute to a clearer picture of student learning? Student-involved methods?

7.3 DEVELOPING MULTIPLE CRITERIA REVISITED

Return to Case 3.4, Developing Multiple Criteria, and reread the case and your response to it. Now that you have completed your study of Chapter 7 on essay assessment, devise an actual set of generic performance criteria for evaluating

- student mastery of the content required for a sound answer to an essay exercise,
- the quality of student reasoning in their responses to an essay exercise, and
- the quality of the writing students use to communicate their ideas.

See if you can devise scoring guides for all three areas that could be applied to student responses to any essay exercise. If you run into difficulty, try to articulate why. Be sure to think carefully about and discuss differences in these kinds of academic achievement.

7.4 ACCOUNTING FOR MORE: WHAT'S THE MATCH BETWEEN THE TASK AND THE CRITERIA?

You're part of a group of middle school teachers scoring student responses to a simple task. The scoring guide uses a continuum that combines numeric scores (5-1) and descriptive words (Exemplary, Proficient, Developing, etc.). As you work, you are beginning to develop mental pictures of the various levels of performance for criteria like Reasoning and Communication. However, another of the criteria/dimensions that you are scoring is the correctness of the answer.

There isn't much of a description for this criterion and at first that doesn't seem to be a problem. As one of the teachers at your table jokes, how can there be degrees of correctness to a correct answer?

Here's the task and two sample responses:[1]

Task: A farmer lost his entire crop. Why might this have happened?

Sample 1
- Drought

Sample 2
- Floods and heavy rains destroyed them.
- Drought destroyed them.
- Was demolished for business construction.
- Went bankrupt, unable to look after his crop.
- Unsuitable soil/land, so the crop died.
- The birds ate all the seeds.

- He didn't take proper care of his crops.
- Unsuitable environment for growing his crops

Initial Reflections

1. What's your initial response to the students' answers?
2. On a scale from 1-5, with 5 being exemplary, what score would you give the answer in the first sample? Why? How would you score the answer in second example? Why?

   Now the case continues:

   It seemed fairly obvious that the second response was a much fuller and more complete answer. Then someone at the table raises the question of whether the exercise communicated clearly to students that multiple reasons were required for an excellent answer. He asks the group to think about the student who provided the first sample.

   "How could we respond if the student pointed out that the question was answered and the answer is correct? I know that some of my students would think it was really unfair to demand more than the task prompts, especially at their age, when they are incredibly sensitive about fairness."

   Another teacher argues that we had to be honest about the quality of the answers. "The first student's answer is OK but not sufficient to be scored exemplary. It isn't even a complete sentence. Any student would know that such a minimal answer is not going to get a high score."

   The first teacher disagrees. "I don't think that the prompt was clear about what would constitute an exemplary answer. If we want students to produce quality work, they need to include enough detail in the task to help them understand what quality work looks like."

   A third teacher calls everyone back to the criteria. "Our rubric isn't fully developed yet. This is an example of what happens when we only have the criteria—we can all interpret them differently and so can the students."

Initial Reflections

1. Is it fair to place one student higher on a continuum of achievement when there was nothing in the prompt that suggested more than one solution would be rewarded? Or should they both get the same score since both provided correct answers? Why?

Discussion Starters

1. What strategies could be used to assure that the criteria for strong responses are clearly understood by students?

2. How closely should the task prompts match the criteria?

3. Would it be better for this group to use task-specific (rather than generic) criteria? What are the advantages? What are the disadvantages?

4. When can we remove mental scaffolding and demand that students understand the requirements of exemplary responses?

Notes

[1]From *A Toolkit for Professional Developers: Mathematics and Science Alternative Assessment* (Portland, Oregon: Laboratory Network Program, Northwest Regional Educational Laboratory, 1995). Reprinted by permission.

8

Performance Assessment: Rich with Possibilities

8.1 A TERM PAPER ASSIGNMENT

The assignment was very clear: *Read four novels by the same author and write a literary term paper arising from that experience. Develop a guiding thesis and use insights derived from your reading to defend your thesis.* The experienced high school English teacher had been covering American literature for decades and had been assigning term papers in this way for as long. It always worked well.

One high school student, an avid reader, had no trouble finding a socially conscious author and searching out and reading four compelling novels about the justices and injustices of our culture. The author was a female and her stories focused on the female experience in United States history—the roles, challenges, and triumphs of women.

However, next came the challenge for our young scholar. She had no confidence as a writer, even though adults in her family had told her that they saw evidence in her work that she could be a talented young writer. She wasn't buying it. What should she do?

The assignment contained no information about the attributes of a good term paper. "Just apply previously learned lessons from other teachers," said her mentor. "This is a term paper like all the others." The problem, however, was that our young writer had received almost no prior instruction in how to organize, let alone compose, such a piece.

Nevertheless, she picked a prominent character from each novel and structured her paper around a comparative analysis of these women. She established the standards of comparison up front and examined key similarities and differences between and among them. To conclude, she used her comparison to speculate about the character and experiences of the woman who had created these characters.

She had to turn the draft in by a specified date or have her grade for the project reduced. She met the deadline, delivered the draft to her teacher, and learned that she wouldn't get it back—after all how could one teacher review 180 drafts! (A valid point—especially when there would be another 180 final versions to read and evaluate later.) But her teacher assured the class that as the final submission deadline approached, they would thank him for requiring the preliminary version.

Over the next two weeks, this student worked to polish her paper. She revised and edited slightly—reading paragraphs to her parents and worrying that it just wasn't good enough. Finally the due date arrived and our young author turned her paper over to her teacher.

Two weeks later, the paper was returned. On the cover, the teacher had written two things: "B+" (certainly a very good grade by most standards, especially for a first big paper) and a single comment: "You used the word 'she' entirely too many times in this paper." There was no other feedback.

Upon returning home, our student showed the paper to her parents. They asked what she herself thought of her efforts. She dropped the paper in the waste basket, wondered aloud what her teacher really thought of her work, said she needn't have wasted so much time worrying or working, and left the room. For her, this product-based performance assessment was a frustrating and unfulfilling experience. How could it have been more productive?

Initial Reflections

1. This teacher found the best way he could to deal with the immense numbers of papers to be read. Was he wrong—given his realities?

2. If you were a student who worked this hard to receive this feedback, how would you react?

Discussion Starters

1. Specifically what went wrong here? List as many problems as you can. Which ones could have been avoided?

2. How might student-involved assessment, recordkeeping, and communication have been used to provide a manageable assessment for the teacher and a more fulfilling experience for this student and her classmates?

8.2 A SCIENCE APPLICATION OF PERFORMANCE ASSESSMENT

A middle school science teacher poses a practical problem for her students to solve that requires the application of their science knowledge and skills: *Given three different kinds of paper towels, determine which absorbs the most liquid and which absorbs the least.* She provides the following materials: a scale for weighing, tweezers, a ruler, three water glasses, a timer, three small dishes, three flat trays, a pitcher of water, two funnels, an eye dropper, and a pair of scissors. The students are asked to keep notebooks describing the procedures they used and their results. Notebook entries are evaluated to determine the students' grades. The teacher's performance scoring and grading scheme appears below, exactly as presented to her students.[1]

HANDS-ON PAPER TOWELS SCORE FORM

Student_____Observer_____Score_____

1. **Method for Getting Towel Wet**

   A. Container: (1) pour water in/put towel in; (2) put towel in/pour water in

   B. Drops

   C. Tray (surface): (1) towel on tray/pour water on; (2) pour water on tray/put towel in

   D. No method

2. **Saturation**

   A. Yes.   B. No.   C. Controlled (same amount of water—all towels)

3. **Determine Result**

   A. Weigh towel

   B. Squeeze towel/measure water (weight or volume)

   C. Measure water in/out

   D. Count # drops until saturated

   E. Irrelevant measurement (i.e., time to soak up water, see how far drops spread out, feel thickness)

   F. Other_____

4. **Care in saturation and/or measuring**

   Yes   No   A little sloppy (+/–)

5. **Correct result**   Most   Least

Grade	Method	Saturate	Determine Result	Care in Measuring	Correct Answers
A	Yes	Yes	Yes	Yes	Both
B	Yes	Yes	Yes	No	One or Both
C	Yes	Controlled	Yes	Yes/No	One or Both
D	Yes	No *or*	Inconsistent	Yes/No	One or Both
F	Inconsis-tent *or*	No *and*	Irrelevant	Yes/No	One or Both

Initial Reflections

1. According to standards of quality performance criteria, is the perform-ance activity sound?
2. Does the task represent clear and complete communication to students?
3. What role might students have played, if any, in developing the as-sessment?

Discussion Starters

1. In your opinion, is this a sound performance assessment rating system? Defend your perspective.
2. Are the grading procedures/standards of high quality? Why or why not?

8.3 SEEKING QUALITY PERFORMANCE CRITERIA

Two different sets of performance criteria are presented below. Please read them.

Example #1

Use these rating scales to evaluate student solutions to complex open-ended math story problems:

A. Formulating/understanding the problem/task, including the identification of assumptions and missing or extraneous data.

1	2	3	4	5
No evidence				Substantial evidence

B. Choosing one or more strategies, including making appropriate modifications or adaptations.

1	2	3	4	5
No evidence			Substantial evidence	

C. Carrying out the procedures, including the appropriate use of technology, models and other resources.

1	2	3	4	5
No evidence			Substantial evidence	

D. Looking back to verify, summarize and/or interpret results.

1	2	3	4	5
No evidence			Substantial evidence	

Example #2

Use these rating scales to evaluate student expository descriptions of the reasoning behind the solutions presented:

A. Expresses the thinking involved in mathematical reasoning, conjecturing, exploring and processing used in the selected piece.

1	2	3	4	5
No evidence			Substantial evidence	

B. Expresses the reflection of the student on the thinking involved in the selected piece.

1	2	3	4	5
No evidence			Substantial evidence	

C. Uses developmentally appropriate mathematical language and notation correctly.

1	2	3	4	5
No evidence			Substantial evidence	

Initial Reflections

1. What standards of quality should we apply in developing scoring criteria?

Discussion Starters

1. Do you see flaws in either? Compare them. Besides the fact that one focuses on the domain of math problem solving and the other on writing descriptions of solutions, are they alike in any ways? Different?

2. If you were charged with revising each set to meet standards of quality criteria, how would you do that?

Notes

[1]From R.J. Shavelson, G.P. Baxter, and J. Pine. "Performance Assessment in Science," *Applied Measurement in Education* 4(4): 347-362. Reprinted by permission.

9

Personal Communication: Another Window to Student Achievement

9.1 ASSESSING INQUIRY: CAN WE USE STUDENT QUESTIONS AS EVIDENCE OF LEARNING?

While working together to connect standards, curriculum, instruction, and assessment, a group of mathematics and science specialists begins to discuss strategies for keeping accurate records when using personal communication.

One of the specialists starts things off: "One of our standards *is* Mathematics As Communication. I can see pretty clearly how to examine students' problem solutions to determine their ability to describe what they did and why, and I could use personal communication to follow up when it's hard to see from their work why they made the choices they did. We've even adapted some criteria to evaluating the quality of mathematical communication. But I'm also interested in what further questions they might have after they've worked on a mathematical investigation that has no single solution. Those questions could be evaluated from a number of different perspectives."

One of the science specialists in the group adds her thoughts: "When it comes to our standard on Science As Inquiry, we're pretty clear on the potential for quality assessment using personal communication—including really good questioning—but I don't want teachers to be the ones asking all the questions. Inquiry is not just about teachers' questions. It's about students posing their own questions and using the tools and habits of mind of the scientist to pursue answers. My instincts tell me it would be really valuable to track the kinds of questions our students are raising themselves—and some of the best ones come right in the midst of teaching. How do we keep track? And how can we categorize the questions?"

Others, picking up on the idea added their thoughts:

"Do you think students' questions will get more and more sophisticated as the year progresses or as students move from grade to grade?"

"What does that mean? What would it sound like? Are there key ideas or even words that we can track?"

"Maybe the science they focus on will get more complex, or will the questions get more complex—deeper?"

"Is it the same thing?"

"Can't we also look at the kinds of thinking skills they are using as they pose questions?"

"I'm not sure how to track the kinds of questions our students raise."

The discussion closes with agreement that recording the questions that students raise would provide valuable evidence about the growth of scientific inquiry skills and useful direction for instruction as students pursue mathematical investigations. But the teachers are uncertain how best to manage and document students' growth in terms of the questions they raise and pursue.

Discussion Starters

1. What advice would you give this group?
2. What recordkeeping strategies might provide useful information for assessment?
3. How might students be involved in documenting their questions?
4. What cautions would you suggest to minimize the possibility of inaccurate assessment?
5. How would you use the information gathered about students' questions?

9.2 THE CASE FOR AND AGAINST PARTICIPATION GRADES

The school district ad hoc committee on grading and report cards has been charged with recommending new grading policies to the school board. One topic of intense discussion is the basis upon which grades should be assigned. All agree that student achievement should be the primary factor. But a debate has emerged about the appropriateness of others.

One teacher holds that participation in class should be a factor: "How can I conduct class discussions if I don't attach some rewards and punishments to contributing to those discussions?"

"But," a colleague challenges, "what if the student is simply too shy to speak up? Is that convincing evidence of a lack of achievement?"

"Look, one of life's important lessons is that you speak up or get left out. I can force such students out of that shyness. It's part of my job as a teacher. Talk or see your grade lowered," says a veteran of many years.

Finally the only first year teacher on the staff pipes up. "I have students who aren't proficient with English. Besides, some are newly arrived in the U.S. from cultures in which children are neither to be seen nor heard. What's fair for them when it comes to grading?"

"Yeah," says a supporter of the idea of counting participation, "but I teach social studies—civics—and one lesson I must teach is how to participate in a democracy. I interpret that to mean participating in public debates about timely issues. It's one of my skill targets for my students."

Another teacher adds, "Well, but who controls who gets to contribute to the discussion? Student or teacher? Obviously, the teacher does. So is it fair to hold students accountable for something they do not control? Besides, how do you keep records of rate or quality of participation so everyone is treated fairly? Oh, and what is it supposed to be—rate or quality—anyway?"

The argument rages on for fifteen minutes, point and counterpoint. Finally it is time for the committee to make its recommendation about relying on assessments of student participation to arrive at a report card grade. What should the committee recommend and why?

Initial Reflections

1. Review each of the points raised above. Does each have merit?
2. Upon what criteria should this judgment be based?

Discussion Starters

1. What should the policy be—consider participation in grading or not? Why?

9.3 *EVALUATING TEACHER PERFORMANCE IN THE AREA OF EFFECTIVE QUESTIONING*

A principal sits at her desk pondering an assessment challenge. She wants to devise a classroom observation scheme to evaluate the questioning skills of her teachers. She knows that effective questioning during instruction can be a very helpful form of classroom assessment. She also knows that it can be done well or poorly. She wants to be sure her teachers are doing it well, so she wants to evaluate their performance.

Further, she wants her observations, evaluations, and feedback to help her teachers become more effective questioners. Certainly they should be held accountable for doing a good job in the classroom, but she also wants her observation results to serve formative purposes.

Based on what you know about sound classroom questioning practice as described in Chapter 9 and what you know about sound performance assessment design as described in Chapter 8, develop a classroom observation scheme that this principal could use to gather data on the questioning strategies of her teachers.

Initial Reflections

1. As you think about this task, be sure to bear in mind the target—effective questioning—and remain constantly aware that the principal will rely on performance assessment methodology to gather data on teacher performance. Our five standards of quality assessment practice must be observed, even when principals are evaluating teachers.

Discussion Starters

1. How should this administrator evaluate the questioning skills of her faculty members?

10

Assessing Reasoning

10.1 THE DILEMMA OF MULTIPLE TARGETS

Two samples of writing are presented below. Students were asked to write a convincing essay in which they justify their preference for a particular type of music. They were to support their arguments with reasons and evidence, considering criteria, analyzing in terms of those criteria, and offering evidence in support of their points of view.

Please read the first sample of writing and then, *before reading on,* answer this question: In your opinion, is the sample well written? You might apply the six analytical writing assessment score scales presented in Chapter 8, page 182.

> *"Well, you're getting to the age when you have to learn to be responsible!" my mother yelled out.*
>
> *"Yes, but I can't be available all the time to do my appointed chores! I'm only thirteen! I want to be with my friends, to have fun! I don't think that it is fair for me to baby-sit while you go run your little errands!" I snapped back. I sprinted upstairs to my room before my mother could start another sentence. I turned on my radio and "Shout" was playing. I noted how true the song was and I threw some punches at my pillow. The song ended and "Control" by Janet Jackson came on. I stopped beating my pillow. I suddenly felt at peace with myself. The song had slowed me down. I pondered briefly over all the songs that had helped me to control my feelings. The list was endless. So is my devotion to rock music and pop rock. The songs help me to express my feelings, they make me wind down, and above all they make me feel good. Without music, I might have turned out to be a violent and grumpy person.*

Some of my favorite songs are by Howard Jones, Pet Shop Boys, and Madonna. I especially like songs that have a message in them, such as "Stand by Me" by Ben E. King. This song tells me to stand by the people I love and to not question them in times of need. Basically this song is telling me to believe in my friends, because they are my friends.

My favorite type of music is rock and pop rock. Without them, there is no way that I could survive mentally. They are with me in times of trouble, and best of all, they are only a step away."[1]

After you have thoughtfully evaluated the quality of the writing, please answer this question before reading on: Is this piece well reasoned? As you think about the question, bear in mind the elements of reasoning discussed in Chapter 10, page 272 (on purpose, central problem, etc.). Go back and review them if necessary. Also remember those dimensions of each element that might be the subject of our evaluation (clarity, relevance, etc.).

Now please read this second sample of student writing and determine if it is well written and if it is well reasoned.

It's certainly hard to objectively judge music based on justifiable criteria because most people don't have any real standards for the music they listen to other than they like it. My friends and I are probably not different from other people. We listen to music we like because we like it. But this assignment asks me to give good reasons why we like what we like. I'm not sure I can, but I'll try.

I first wonder what would be a really good reason for liking any kind of music (other than it sounds good to you). Well, I suppose that one possible good reason for preferring one kind of music to another is that it expresses better the problems we face and what we can do to solve those problems.

Does this give me a good reason for preferring rock music to other kinds? Perhaps so. Certainly, rock music is often about problems we have: problems of love and sex, school and parents, drugs and drinking. I'm not sure, however, whether the "answers" in the songs actually are really good answers or just answers that appeal to us. They might even increase our prejudices about parents, teachers, school and love. I'm not sure.

Another possible good reason for preferring one kind of music to another is that it is written better or more skillfully performed. Can I truthfully say that rock music is more skillfully written or performed than other kinds of music? In all honesty, I cannot.

So what is my conclusion? It is this. I am unable to give any objective reasons for liking rock music. My friends and I are like most people. We like the music we listen to because we like it. For better or for worse, that's all the reason we have. What do you think? Can 15 million teenagers be wrong?[2]

Initial Reflections

Compare these two pieces of work:

1. Is one written better than the other?
2. Is one more powerfully reasoned than the other? How do you know?

Discussion Starters

1. When a student has written a response to an essay question, a teacher can evaluate that work using any of three different sets of performance criteria. The response can be evaluated in terms of the student's mastery of the content, the quality of his or her writing, or the quality of the reasoning used. How should a teacher decide which set of standards to apply?
2. What are likely to be the essential differences among those different sets of criteria? What will be the trade offs when we choose one set of criteria over the others?
3. How might you use reasoning criteria to help students deliver quality performance according to those standards?

10.2 EVALUATING THE QUALITY OF REASONING

An editorial from a daily newspaper appears on the next page. Please read it carefully.[3]

Discussion Starters

1. In your opinion, is the editorial well reasoned? On what criteria do you base your judgment? Be specific.

10.3 A SOUND ASSESSMENT OF REASONING?

Return to Case 6.2, The Challenge of Fixing a Troubled Test, and reread the case (instructional unit, table of specifications, test exercises) and your reactions to the assessment from a quality-control point of view. In your original reflections did you comment on the test as an assessment of student reasoning? The table of specifications says it is supposed to be just that. Now that you have completed your study of Chapter 10 on the assessment of rea-

Closing the drive-through

*Plan requiring coverage of hospital stays
offers new mothers and babies a better start*

Mother and baby are doing well.

Welcome words — and now chances are better that they will remain true. House and Senate negotiators Thursday announced agreement on legislation requiring insurance companies to pay for at least 48 hours in the hospital for mothers giving birth.

New mothers in the United States stay in the hospital after delivering their babies for the shortest time of any in the world. Between 1970 and 1992, the median hospital stay declined from 3.9 to 2.1 days for a vaginal delivery and from 7.8 to 4 days for a Caesarean section, according to the Centers for Disease Control and Prevention.

While this trend began with wider recognition that childbirth is a natural process and not an illness, it accelerated, and became dangerous in some cases, as a part of increased health care cost-containment efforts. Many insurers now require mothers to leave the hospital 12 to 24 hours after an uncomplicated birth.

This practice, while indeed saving money, is dangerous because some problems for mothers and babies aren't immediately apparent. Newborns face threats such as jaundice, infection and dehydration from failure to properly breastfeed, and new mothers face complications such as hemorrhage and stroke. Hospitals can provide monitoring and education in skills such as bathing, feeding and spotting trouble that not every new mother can easily obtain from home.

The bill requires coverage of 48-hour stays for normal vaginal deliveries and 96-hour stays following Caesarean sections — time periods that conform to guidelines of the American College of Obstetricians and Gynecologists and the American Academy of Pediatrics. This is a reasonable cushion to make sure that there are no complications for the mother or child. Return emergency room or hospital visits that result from drive-through deliveries are not good for patients or insurers.

Twenty-eight states (but not Oregon) have passed similar legislation, and a CDC study of four New Jersey hospitals following enactment of its law in June 1995 found that mothers whose deliveries were normal stayed in the hospital 10 to 12 hours longer.

The bill does not prevent a woman and her doctor from deciding she can go home sooner — many women want to, are able to and can get proper follow-up care. But insurers are prohibited from offering incentives to mothers or doctors for doing that.

The government shouldn't get carried away with dictating individual health plan provisions, but it is entirely justified in taking this step that helps ensure mother and baby are doing well.

> **"** *Our members tell us that women are being pressured to leave the hospital early, sometimes in eight hours or less, and physicians are being pressured to discharge their patients before they feel they should go home. If health maintenance organizations had done this voluntarily, we would not have to have new laws.* **"**
>
> **— Dr. Ralph W. Hale,**
> executive director,
> American College of Obstetricians and
> Gynecologists

soning, go back and reevaluate this test. Once again, make adjustments as needed to turn it into a quality assessment of student reasoning.

10.4 QUESTIONING TO LEARN VS. QUESTIONING TO CHALLENGE

This case continues the discussion of a regional group of science specialists in Case 9.1. Nic has raised a nagging concern about student questioning within his culture: "We've been talking about finding good ways to record and track the kinds of questions our students ask and to use those questions to provide insights into student reasoning. That may be fine in some parts of our region, but in my culture it's really inappropriate for young people to be questioning adults. It's very disrespectful."

Nic is one of two dozen Pacific island educators representing ten distinct and separate educational systems, stretched in small clusters of islands across more than 10,000 square miles and at least 15 different language groups. The educators have been working together for more than three years. Coming to agreement on regional standards for excellence in mathematics and science content, teaching, assessment, and professional development has required frequent discussion about the impact and appropriateness of decisions on the realities and values of the multiple cultures represented in the group.

Often, questions like Nic's set off serious discussion and raise the continuing dilemma of how to honor culture while continuing to build learning communities that must respond to other cultures in order to survive. All of the challenges have come together in Nic's question.

Martin is the first to respond. "We have to get away from the idea that students shouldn't question if our young people are going to become scientifically literate. Questioning is central to science and I want our kids to believe they can succeed in the sciences. We need their scientific knowledge and skills for our future. But it's more than having students who are confident and interested in science. Right now I see kids who often wait to be told what to do. They expect the answers to come from outside themselves— even outside their culture. They sometimes don't trust their own reasoning power. Helping them to frame their own questions is a part of making them independent learners. There's more at stake here than tracking the questions that they pose."

Pam adds her thoughts: "We've got to look carefully at how school and home are connected. Parents are unhappy when their children come home and ask questions about why adults are doing things, or decisions they've made. Too often they see school as an alien culture, completely separate from their lives. They worry that their children will lose their culture. How can we be respectful of the culture and also carry out the standards we've set? They describe goals that demand independent thinking, mathematical and scientific reasoning, questioning, analyzing, and much more. Our elders are deeply concerned that their children are losing sight of what's important in their culture. They're not being as respectful as they should be. Our encouragement of questioning may be seen as challenging the roles and authority of not just parents."

Bernie has been listening carefully. She offers her thoughts: "Maybe we can make a distinction between questioning to learn and questioning to challenge. If we can separate the two, and our students can see that there's a difference—and their parents, too—then we might be able to balance between what we value in science and the respect that's central in our culture."

Martin concurs: "A good scientist is always questioning and seeking to weigh what's known with new information. Scientists question for a purpose. Our students need to have opportunities for the kinds of thinking that scientists do. If they can become conscious of the kinds of thinking necessary for scientific inquiry—and can do it well—we'll be on our way."

Philo adds some ideas from his experience: "We need to educate the parents, to involve them in some of the same kinds of activities. I've been working with parents on family math and it's really made a difference."

Aurelio reminds the group that there's much to be learned from parents. "Our history and some of our practices come from careful observation and quiet inquiry in our cultures. Our traditional medicines and navigation are filled with good scientific knowledge. There has to be a way to connect the scientist's ways of reasoning and our culture."

Initial Reflections

1. As you think about this case, what are the key facts? How do you feel about the distinction that these educators are seeking to make? Although this group represents Pacific island cultures, are there experiences of your own or of your students that pose similar concerns? What information and ideas in Chapter 10 can provide some guidance?

Discussion Starters

1. What assessment questions does this case pose?
2. How could this group build bridges between the questioning that is part of the scientific inquiry process and questioning that is designed to undermine and challenge authority in the culture?
3. What strategies would you suggest for this group as it approaches parents and the community about its science standards? What barriers do you envision? Brainstorm some possible pathways around the barriers.

4. How might increased knowledge of assessing reasoning contribute to this group's work? To parents' perception of the purposes of questioning in science?

5. What questions remain unanswered?

Notes

[1]California Department of Education, 1988, as presented in Richard Paul, *Critical Thinking* (Santa Rosa, California: Foundation for Critical Thinking, 1995), p. 172. Used by permission.

[2]Paul, p. 176.

[3]*The Oregonian*, Portland, Oregon, September 24, 1996. Reprinted by permission.

11

Performance Assessments of Skill and Product Targets

11.1 TWO FOR THE PRICE OF ONE? ASSESSING READING AND WRITING TOGETHER

I (Kathy) am still mulling over a recent experience that raised questions in my mind about the degree to which we can use students' writings as reflections of their reading proficiency. Do we consider reading and writing together in our assessments? Can they or should they be viewed separately within a single task? Should we attempt to unravel the woven strands to examine which elements of a student's response give us clear pictures of their writing skill and which provide insights into their reading proficiency? As we continue to build complex tasks for both instruction and assessment, are we in danger of muddying the vision of our target?

I am a member of a middle school task force working on developing model assessments linked to our state's literacy performance standards. We've got what we consider a strong integrated program and have been focusing on reading and writing across the curriculum. Given this emphasis, we want to use integrated assessments that employ historical text and let us gather useful information about our students' reading and writing proficiency.

To get a clear sense of our target, we began by discussing the things that good readers do and describing their characteristics. In the list we came up with, good readers:

- connect their reading to things they already know
- enjoy reading
- use strategies to understand what they read

- know how to read different kinds of text
- interpret what they read
- can communicate clearly about the text
- understand the content of the text
- use visualization

Then we added the idea of reading historical text and generated some additional characteristics of good readers. We said that they

- understand the historical context
- are able to determine the point of view of the author
- can make connections between the historical period and current times

We wanted to use our assessments to model good reading and writing instruction, as well as quality performance tasks and criteria. The performance task that we created has several steps. We included suggestions to students about jotting down some things they already know about the topic—in this case, child labor. Here's the performance task we developed:

GENERAL INSTRUCTIONS

Read the following pages, which give you some information about child labor in the 1800s. You will be asked to identify the important ideas you have about child labor from this information.

Then you will be asked to imagine that it is the year 1912 and the United States Congress is investigating child labor. A town meeting in your community has been called to examine the issues. Decide whether you believe that it is right or wrong for children to work. Take a firm stand.

You will be providing written testimony expressing your position to citizens, business leaders, and legislators at the town meeting. The town meeting will make decisions about child labor. Your job is to persuade the citizens to accept your point of view on child labor. You should use information from the readings to support your stand.

The final version of your written testimony will be scored on how well your testimony makes sense, the important ideas you included to support your argument, how well you show relationships between your ideas and the readings, and how well you persuade the reader to accept your point of view.

As you read each of the passages you may underline, highlight, or mark directly on the sheet. In the space provided, you may jot down notes on the important ideas presented in the texts.

Think about what it is like to be a child who works. Think about working conditions. Think about what they have and don't have because of their jobs. Try making a list, a web, or a diagram or quickly writing ideas that you got from the readings to come up with your opinion about whether it is right or wrong for children to work.

When we presented this task to a joint meeting of our integrated teaching teams and had the teachers do the task, we were anxious to get their reactions and input for improving both the task and the criteria. At first the teams were engaged and enthusiastic. Discussion about the writing was lively and animated. Then it was time to go back to the characteristics of good readers—and readers of historical text—that we had drafted together earlier.

While some of our brainstormed "characteristics" could be used (ones like "They know how to use a variety of strategies to pick out key ideas," and "They can present the ideas in a organized way"), others seemed out of sync with the purposes of the task. Much discussion focused on the persuasiveness of the writing, and additional descriptions for our criteria began to emerge:

- has structure and logic
- has assumptions that are supported in the text
- evokes emotion with the argument and details
- establishes a relationship between the writer's own ideas and the readings
- presents an extended argument using supporting examples
- takes a point of view and defends it
- avoids using details that detract from the argument
- supports a point of view with evidence and examples
- makes a personal commitment to the point of view clearly

When the group noted that one criterion provided with the task called for assessment of the extent to which the writer used information from the texts, there was some concern.

Was it the quality of the persuasive writing that we were assessing? If so, wasn't it possible to do a fine job without referring frequently to the text? Wouldn't the nature of the final product call for the writer to appeal to emotions as well as intellect? Did the number of text citations contribute to the persuasiveness, or could it perhaps dilute the power of the arguments? Does persuasive writing rely on logic and the piling up of details, or can it build on exaggeration and emotion? These questions began to take us away from examining the product as a record of reading—as an assessment of reading as well as writing.

The group began to question what insights could be gained about the reading of historical text when the task has a piece of persuasive writing as its final product. Several participants contributed ideas about the characteristics of good writing to the discussion and the group struggled some more to come up with a not very satisfying set of characteristics that included some from reading criteria and some from writing criteria.

The thoughtfulness and care needed to create quality performance assessments became very clear, but I was still left with nagging questions about how well we had defined our assessment targets—and with serious concerns about whether "real" students who read and understand the text samples might score poorly because of their writing skills. Didn't we need to examine more than that final product? Are the two—reading and writing— so much a whole, as many believe, that they shouldn't be separated in assessment? What options do we have to create a much clearer picture of the learning related to each target? How could the task itself be modified and improved?

Initial Reflections

1. Are there connections between facets of this case and your own experiences? What elements of the case echo problems you have faced? Did you respond differently? Are there insights from your experience that can be brought to a discussion of this case?

Discussion Starters

1. The questions below should be part of your case discussion. Use your reading in this chapter and others, as well as your practical experience with performance assessment, to consider them:

- Was the performance to be evaluated *clear*?
- Was it clear what an assessor will be examining or observing to determine reading proficiency?
- Should the task be broken into parts with different targets for each part?
- How would you change the directions and the actual tasks to further emphasize that this task is an assessment of both reading and writing?
- Do you think there are biases built into the task when the overall assessment is based on the written product? Whose learning might be masked?
- How would you expand the criteria? Would you use separate scoring guides for reading and writing? Why? Why not?
- What elements need more work? What specific suggestions would you make to improve the quality of the assessments?
- Can you really get two for one with this task? How would you report the learning?

11.2 ALIGNING INSTRUCTION AND ASSESSMENT

Below is a draft unit of instruction developed by a team of science teachers.[1] It includes information about achievement expectations, instructions to students, and assessment. Please read it and then discuss this case.

INSTRUCTIONAL UNIT/ PERFORMANCE TASKS

Unit Focus: Weather in the Marshall Islands; Grades 5 and 6

Academic Standard

Students will be able to use scientific process (exploring, observing, investigating, comparing, etc.), knowledge, and reasoning to illustrate their understanding of science.

Learning Targets

Observe, record, discuss weather patterns, temperature, wind direction, cloud patterns, and measure precipitation.

Infer connections among rainfall, wind speed, cloud patterns, wind direction, and temperature.

Assignment to Students

You're going to be part of a weather reporting team whose data can help get a clearer picture of weather patterns around your island. If you carefully collect, analyze, and report your weather data, your findings will be included in a national radio broadcast. Each team will observe, measure, and record information. Together you will pool your data to look for patterns and relationships between things like wind speed and direction, rainfall, cloud formations, and temperature. Some of your data will be gathered by observation, some will involve the careful and accurate use of measurement tools.

Gather Data:

Twice daily (in morning and afternoon), observe and record (draw and label) cloud patterns outside your classroom.

Set up a rain gauge when you do your morning cloud observations and record actual rainfall toward the end of the afternoon.

Set up an anemometer and a wind vane and record wind direction and wind speed in the morning and afternoon.

Keep a record of each day's temperature (morning and afternoon) with a thermometer.

Graph your data on rainfall, wind speed, and temperature after two weeks of observations and record-keeping. Continue gathering and adding to your records throughout the time set by your teacher (can be up to one full school year).

Keep a daily log/journal in which you record your data, your reactions, possible patterns that are emerging, and notes on the specific part that you've had in collecting data with your group.

Talk with older family or community members about their knowledge of weather patterns and relationships. Are there stories about the weather that they remember? Ask about other things which can indicate changes in weather patterns.

Ask about trends in weather around your island that elders remember from their youth. Do they see any significant changes?

Analyze Your Data:

Describe any weather patterns you see that might connect specific cloud forms with the amount of rainfall (at least one person in the group should record cloud patterns whenever it rains).

Is there any relationship (describe) between wind direction and the weather the next day?

Describe any relationships/patterns you observe that might connect temperature with the cloud forms or rainfall and weather patterns. (Any patterns between drops or increases in temperature and rainfall? Or bad weather?)

Are there any clear relationships between wind speed or pressure and temperature? Specific cloud formations? Rainfall?

Check your findings with family or community elders to see if they are consistent with traditional weather knowledge.

Report Findings:

Prepare a written report and present your findings to the whole class. Use drawings, photos, graphs, and/or tables in your report. Record a summary for use on the radio.

Each person in your group must take part in the oral report and be ready to answer questions about any part of your group's work.

Include information gathered from family and community in your report; note where your data confirmed traditional knowledge of weather.

Assessment Plan

The team believed that this instructional activity also afforded an excellent opportunity to assess student achievement. They summarized their assessment plan as follows:

Assessment Methods:

- Performance Assessment
  - —Observing during data collection
  - —Examining products (science logs, data recording sheets, graphs, tables, etc.)
  - —Observing presentations of findings
- Paper/Pencil Items (Selected Response)
  - —Checking knowledge of weather terms and conditions using multiple choice items
- Personal Communication
  - —Questioning students about processes, data interpretation, findings
  - —Listening to group discussions while students are gathering, interpreting and preparing to report
- Essay
  - —Reviewing the reports of each group

Assessment Criteria:

- Observations
  - —Accuracy
  - —Correct weather features observed
- Data Interpretation
  - —Analysis of appropriate data
  - —Generalizations are backed by the data
  - —Inability to generalize is identified where data do not support any generalization
- Record Keeping
  - —Accuracy
  - —Detail
- Communication/Reporting
  - —Presentation
  - —Clear, appropriate terms used
  - —Visuals supporting the reported data
- Cooperation/Team Work
  - —Everyone contributes to the data collection, analysis, and reporting
  - —Members share ideas and reach agreement on findings
  - —Group members are prepared and take responsibility for their part in the weather reporting

Initial Reflections

1. What assessment opportunities does this unit offer?

2. What kinds of assessment methods seem to fit those opportunities? Can you fill in some details regarding how the methods listed might come into play?

3. Do you think the performance criteria section of the plan is sufficiently detailed? How might it be amplified to include more detail?

Discussion Starters

1. If you were to implement this instructional plan, what specific assessment plan would you use to evaluate student achievement?

2. What role might students play in that plan—as monitors of their own achievement?

11.3 CRITERIA FOR COLLABORATION

The faculty of an elementary school decides to develop a school-wide cooperative learning environment. To support the effort, teachers devise a student-friendly version of a set of performance criteria on effective collaboration. Those rating scales are presented below.[2]

COLLABORATION/COOPERATION STANDARDS

A. I work to help achieve the goals of the group.

4   I participate actively and even help lead the group in setting goals. I do the jobs assigned to me better than anyone expects.

3   I participate in group discussions and show that I care about the group goals. I complete the jobs assigned to me.

2   I participate in group discussions and show that I care about the group goals, but I do not do the jobs assigned to me.

1   I don't participate in group discussions or show that I care about the group goals; or I actually work against the goals.

B. I communicate well with other group members.

4   I encourage good communication among the group members and try to make sure everyone shares their ideas. When I share my ideas, I show

that I care about other people's feelings and ideas, and I encourage everyone in the group to do the same.

3   I participate in group discussions without being asked to. When I share my ideas, I show that I care about other people's feelings and ideas.

2   I participate in group discussions when I am asked to. When I share my ideas, I don't clearly show that I care about the feelings and ideas of others.

1   I do not participate in group discussions, even when asked to. I share ideas in a way that shows I don't really care about the feelings and ideas of others.

C.   I help make sure the group works well together.

4   I encourage the group to evaluate how well we are working together. I try to get everyone involved in thinking of ways to make changes when we need to improve. When we decide to make changes, I try to make sure the changes help us work better together.

3   I participate in discussions of how well we are working together and help develop suggestions for changes when we need to improve. I work on making the changes that we agree to.

2   I participate in discussions of how well we are working together only when I am asked to, and I don't have ideas for ways to change. When we decide to change, I put little effort into making those changes.

1   I do not participate in discussing how well we are working together. When the group decides to change, I refuse to help work on the changes.

D.   I perform a variety of jobs in my group.

4   I perform many jobs in my group and do them all well.

3   I perform two jobs in my group and do both well.

2   I try to perform two jobs in my group but don't perform both well.

1   I don't even try to perform any more than one job in my group.

Discussion Starters

1. By standards of quality performance criteria established in the text, did these teachers do a good job?

2. Are students likely to understand these criteria?

3. Will they be able to reach them and know when they have?

4. How might these criteria be improved?

5. How might they be most effectively shared with students? With their parents?

6. How might these teachers effectively involve students in developing these criteria?

Notes

[1]From Republic of the Marshall Islands Assessment Coaching Phase II, June 1996. Work in progress. Used by permission.

[2]From R. Marzano, D. Pickering, and J. McTighe, *Assessing Student Outcomes* (Alexandria, Virginia: Association for Supervision and Curriculum Development, 1993). Used by permission.

12

Assessing Student Dispositions

12.1 HABITS OF MIND IN THE ARTS: DO YOU WANT ME TO TELL YOU WHAT YOU THINK, OR DO YOU WANT TO KNOW WHAT I THINK?

Note: This case can be discussed in several rounds. There are reflection and case discussion questions at several points in the presentation. You can choose to wait until you have read the complete case or divide your discussion into several steps spread out over time.

Round 1: Checking the Targets

As the school year has passed, art teachers who struggled early in the year to define the artist's habits of mind have involved their students in building a rubric that could be used across many projects and art forms to portray the habits of mind and dispositions that are developing. It's now late in the school year. An assessment specialist is revisiting the art department of this secondary school. Looking around the classroom, she sees lots of evidence of the students' developing artistic skills. On one wall are scale drawings of various student proposals for a new science and technology center. On another wall, charcoal and pastel drawings catch the eye. In the center of a third wall, a chart with multicolored writing is displayed. Moving closer, the specialist can make out the original Habits of Mind poster, which now has descriptions that students have added over the past few months:

THE ARTIST'S HABITS OF MIND[1]

Persistence

♦   Spending a lot of time
♦   Putting learning effort into it
♦   Doing it until you get it right
♦   Continue in spite of problems
♦   Remain calm and focused on your project
♦   Put a lot of effort into it
♦   Don't give up, keep trying
♦   Work on it until it's perfect in your eyes
♦   Pass your own limits to complete it
♦   Follow your vision not just taking what the teacher gives you
♦   Have the integrity to stay with your idea

Craftsmanship

♦   Developing details in work
♦   Neatness
♦   Connect with caring passionately and persistence
♦   Smoothness when smoothness is needed
♦   Surface texture is appropriate to the idea you intended to develop
♦   Develop texture which represents hair in an authentic way

Problem Solving

♦   Thinking "outside the box"
♦   Using scientific method
♦   Use what you know and gather information and try possible solutions and develop one fully and evaluate
♦   Drawing techniques that make it realistic such as shading/proportion
♦   Trying a couple of different things to make it look right
♦   Working out problems in the sketchbook
♦   Figuring out how to make a specific expression on the face
♦   Decide what you want to do and follow through

Caring Passionately

♦   Thinking about it all the time
♦   Love your work

Collaboration

♦   Asking others' opinions
♦   Group problem solving

- ◆ Working together on a problem/project
- ◆ Putting ideas together (every idea) to make it the best
- ◆ Hear what people say—be quiet enough to hear/listen
- ◆ Responding by rephrasing, asking questions, giving input
- ◆ Express ideas—everyone—get everyone to share; ask people what they think
- ◆ Be attentive; look at the person; don't interrupt
- ◆ Don't put people down
- ◆ Be honest

Being Aware of the Choices You Make

- ◆ Reflecting about why you do things in a certain way
- ◆ Making sure that all of the habits of mind are working to make the best composition

Putting Together Seemingly Unrelated Things

- ◆ Writing related to the way you use clay
- ◆ Connecting a story by juxtaposing different heads
- ◆ Developing of clay busts
- ◆ Developing ideas for dialog

Risk Taking

- ◆ Choosing something that is a challenge
- ◆ Trying out a medium or method that is new (unfamiliar)
- ◆ Experimenting with new ideas

Initial Reflections

1. What are your immediate reactions to the evolving habits of mind targets?
2. Are there some other descriptions that you'd like to add? Questions or concerns?
3. Are the descriptions all at the same level of generality?

   You may choose to begin your case discussion at this point or build your personal reflections and engage in a wide-ranging discussion when the whole case is completed.

Discussion Starters

1. Are the targets clear enough for quality assessment? What else would help?

2. Which descriptions are clear enough to be used by others?

3. Are there some that don't seem to fit?

4. How would you define "risk taking"?

5. If this were your class, in what ways would you gather information or evidence to enable you and your students to make good judgments about the quality of their current habits of mind?

Round 2: Using the Language of Habits of Mind

One teacher talks about what happened when she began to focus attention on habits of mind. She comments that at first she was pleased to see the language of the evolving habits of mind rubric appearing in her students' sketchbooks and journal reflections. They had spent time gradually building examples to clarify each of the habits of mind. In some of their descriptions, they showed real insight. After a while, however, she started to worry that some students were parroting the words to be sure they'd receive points toward their overall art grade. She fretted that the purpose of having students contribute their ideas to the habits of mind rubric was to prompt real insights, not the self-conscious use of set phrases. She was also concerned about whether the habits of mind that were originally identified were the essential artist's habits of mind. And she says, "I can't imagine that we'll ever be done developing this rubric!"

As we talk, the teacher returns to the original issue for her: grading. She had begun this large undertaking with the concern that assessment in her classroom was too narrowly focused on products. The only other factor considered in grading was "neatness," something she found very easy to judge but definitely "inconsequential." As the students explored habits of mind, however, more questions arose.

The teacher became concerned that using student-reported habits of mind evidence in grading was turning attention away from honest self-reflection. At the same time, she felt that assessing habits of mind was important for communicating their value to her students. "Is it possible to assess habits of mind or other dispositions without creating artificial student responses or actions? I want them to dig deeply inside and be thoughtful about the habits of mind that they are developing. What I don't want is a rerun of the old game of them trying to figure out what I want them to say—I want it to be in their own voice. The game seemed to take over for some when I required that they describe growth in each of the habits of mind for credit. After a while I had them pick out five that they thought were important in their current work. But the specter of grading keeps haunting the results."

One of the other teachers concurs: "At first, it was kind of bogus. We talked about risk taking, but some of the things students chose to identify as risks were very minimal. They had little sense of the degree of risk taking in the choices they were making. Now that I've decided not to grade risk taking any more, I've started to see more about it in their reflections."

Continuing Reflections

1. What might happen if this teacher removed the grading credit from students' documentation of their growing habits of mind?

Discussion Starters

1. Do you think that the students' conscious use of the language of habits of mind is, as the teacher fears, a response to please her or a game to ensure points toward a grade? Or could it be part of the process of learning and beginning to own the rubric?

2. How would you encourage students to gradually develop and reveal more insights as they get comfortable with the rubric?

3. What's needed here to make for confident and accurate judgment about a student's habits of mind?

4. How would you deal with habits of mind in grading? Why?

Round 3: Dispositions: How About Collaboration?

Another issue bubbles to the surface. The teacher and her colleagues at their last meeting had begun to reconsider their original list of habits of mind. Student reflections on collaborative group projects had prompted a rethinking about the inclusion of collaboration. When asked "How did collaboration work for you?" a number of students wrote about how hard it was to bring together all of their ideas and very different personalities. The teacher wondered whether the work of an artist, the pursuit of a vision, could actually be blunted and minimized by forced collaboration. Were there some students whose talents required independent and solitary action? Did collaboration belong in the artist's habits of mind? And yet, the world requires teamwork. How do we teach them to hear and consider the unpopular idea or opinion and to determine how to bring out everyone's contributions to a project?

Discussion Starters

1. How would you address the concerns raised about collaboration? Do you see an inconsistency between collaboration and artistic expression?

2. Should all dimensions of a rubric get scored each time the rubric is used? Why? Why not?

3. Would you recommend individual or group grades for collaboration? Both? Why? Why not?

Round 4: Evolving Rubrics

During a final meeting just before the end of school, the teachers pool their experience to draft a revised list of habits of mind with some descriptions. One of their decisions is to build on the power of visual metaphors to create meaning for students. Once again, they plan to involve students in the process. "Part of the learning from this first year was that we didn't have clear enough distinctions—how to separate one habit of mind from another," they thought. The new school year will begin with the following:

Taking Risks

- Use the "jumping in the water" or "diving off a cliff" metaphor. How risky was it? Are you putting your toe in the water or jumping into the wave at Diamond Head? Where are you in the range of risks?
- What's the value of the risk?

Identifying Questions and Seeking Solutions

Being Aware of Choices Being Made

- By keeping a journal of reflections.
- This can include awareness of the cultural context.

Making Connections

- Use a metaphor.
- Have you made enough connections to create a
      group?
      neighborhood?
      town?
- Or are you connecting in many and varied ways like a metropolis?

Creating a Personal, Unique Expression

Collaborating

Discussion Starters

1. Is this set of standards better or worse than those identified in Round 1? Are these teachers making progress? How do you know?

2. How would you assess the habits of mind they are trying to define?

12.2 THE EVALUATION COMMITTEE

A team of teachers at your middle school has decided to apply for a National Science Foundation grant to do action research on new and innovative ways to teach science. You plan to compare three types of instruction to see which is most effective with your student population. At least part of the student body in your school will participate in each of these kinds of science teaching:

1. *Text-based instruction,* in which students learn content from reading the district-adopted textbook and completing text-embedded assignments. Assessment is based on unit, mid-term, and final exams.

2. *Discovery instruction,* in which students develop their understanding of scientific principles by experimenting with ideas in an exploratory lab setting and preparing periodic lab reports to represent their scientific reasoning.

3. *Science and technology in society,* in which students come to understand science as it plays out in the process of finding solutions to real-world problems, such as those related to preserving the environment. Study-team presentations and written reports serve as the basis for evaluation.

Your particular action-planning team has been given the assignment of devising a plan for evaluating the differing impacts of these forms of instruction on student attitudes about science and the study of science. Your research question is, "Which method or methods promotes the strongest positive attitudes—most positive dispositions about learning science?"

More specifically, you must find a way or ways to assess the science dispositions of all 500 students at your middle school. And you must track those feelings as they evolve throughout the school year, starting with beginning dispositions and seeing if they change over time due to the method of instruction used. How will you do this?

Initial Reflections

1. What kinds of affect will you assess?
2. Reflecting on Table 12-2 on page 339 in the text, which method(s) may be most useful? Why?
3. Might you rely on more than one method?

Discussion Starters

1. What steps would you take in building an assessment plan?
2. What are key components of your assessment plan?
3. How might you involve students in this process?

Notes

[1]See Chapter 3 in Carol Iacovelli, *Habits of Mind* (Honolulu, 1995). A work in progress. Used by permission.

13

Classroom Perspectives on Standardized Testing

13.1 THE PROBLEM OF TEXTBOOK SELECTION

A fourth grade teacher confesses to a problem:

"I've just been assigned to a textbook selection committee for elementary science. We met three weeks ago Tuesday to decide what we wanted in a new text series. We put together a set of criteria for evaluating the possibilities. Then we invited representatives from the various publishers to meet with us to review their books. We met two reps two weeks ago and two more last week. Half way through the meeting last Tuesday, it suddenly hit me. We weren't asking any questions about the nature or quality of the assessments that come with the books! What if we adopted a new text series that included bad tests, or worse, offered no tests at all?!

"The reason this question arose was that the fourth representative offered us two options for assessments. We could either buy a set of pre-published chapter and unit tests for use in class or we could buy a computerized test item bank and assemble our own tests. The former is pretty rigid, but cheap. The latter costs a lot of money but is very flexible! After the rep left, I realized two things. First, we had no idea how to choose between the two. Second, this was the first representative to even raise the topic of assessments. We knew nothing about the assessments accompanying the other books.

"Then, to top it off, this last rep shared a thoughtful and thought-provoking analysis of the relationship between her text and the commonly used standardized tests. She asked which test we used. We told her. It turns out that the things our test addresses and the material covered by her text series didn't line up very well from grade to grade. But what about the alignment of our test with the other texts? We didn't even know enough to ask the other reps."

Initial Reflections

1. This teacher and his selection team have painted themselves into a corner. Two issues need resolution. Collect some thoughts about each before discussing this case.

2. What should they do about evaluating the quality of the various assessment options connected to each text?

3. And what should they do to assure the best possible alignment with a standardized test?

Discussion Starters

1. If they were to devise a set of questions to ask each of the other reps on follow up, in order to evaluate the assessment components of their texts, what should those questions be?

2. How could the committee evaluate the match between the various texts and their standardized tests?

3. If committee members were to contact the other reps to glean information about the match of their texts to the various standardized tests on the market, what questions should they ask?

4. If they found a great text, one that reflected their achievement target priorities far better than the others, but also found that it did not overlap at all well with the standardized test the district is now using, should they pass on it or urge that the test be changed?

13.2 THE CONFUSING STANDARDIZED TEST AND ITS RESULTING SCORES

The school district has decided to update its standardized testing program, so a committee is formed to review available tests and see which ones might fit best into the local curriculum.

Upon initial investigation, the committee learns from the local testing company representatives that the tests assess students' mastery of content knowledge and their ability to use that knowledge to reason effectively. That's good, the committee members think, because these targets are key targets to their curriculum frameworks.

As their inquiry proceeds, however, team members begin to uncover some apparent reasons for concern. For example, since the tests are relatively short, given the broad categories of content tested, only a small fraction of the material they teach would be sampled in actual items. What if their curriculum just happened to emphasize material not selected in the sample of questions asked? Or, even worse, what if the test tested content not covered in instruction or covered later in the year? There seemed to be a very high probability that these things could happen. If they did, would the test be considered "fair"? Is it fair to hold students and teachers accountable for being masters of material not covered? Would the test scores still be interpretable? The results useful?

As the rest of the committee deliberates on these issues, one member begins to sense a different potential problem. The test user's guides said all the items assess reasoning proficiency. In a recent workshop on that topic, she learned that the assessment of reasoning requires the presentation of novel questions at the time of the test—questions that students have to figure out on the spot. But what if the published test includes "reasoning test items" that some teachers had actually and explicitly covered in class? These items wouldn't test reasoning power at all—they would test recall of previously learned material. What would this situation mean for test scores? Could they still be interpreted? Could the district still use them?

Discussion Starters

1. Are these legitimate concerns on the part of this committee? Why or why not? What, if anything, can or should they do about them:

- In deciding which test to buy and use?
- In interpreting and using test results?

13.3 KELLY AND THE READING TEST

Kelly recently arrived at Lippert Junior High School from another state. During the first week of school, Ms. Mengeling, her eighth grade English teacher, noticed that Kelly was struggling with her class work. She had yet to turn in any assignments, spent a great deal of time daydreaming, and was constantly asking the student next to her for help figuring out what words meant as she read. Kelly always needed to have instructions repeated and was not able to understand what she was reading.

Ms. Mengeling asked Kelly's science and social studies teachers if they sensed any reading problems. They did. The three of them contacted the guidance office to see what they could learn from the academic records Kelly had brought with her.

The only pertinent information they found were scores on a standardized achievement test administered annually over the past five years by Kelly's previous school. The norm-referenced, group-administered test battery included two relevant scores: vocabulary and reading comprehension. The counselor had culled through all of the data and summarized the key material on Kelly's performance for the teachers. All tests offered four option multiple-choice items. Here are her results in grade-equivalent scores:

Grade Level	Test Form	Vocabulary Score (VB)	Reading Comprehension (RC)	National Norm
3	12	2.3	3.2	3.2
4	13	2.1	2.5	4.2
5	14	2.9	3.1	5.2
6	15	4.0	4.1	6.2
7	16	4.1	4.8	7.2

The science teacher noticed a consistent pattern of growth, but Kelly is falling farther and farther behind. When the teachers asked the guidance counselor for help, she provided the conversion tables for determining grade-equivalent scores on each of the test forms of the particular test battery Kelly took. Those tables follow "Discussion Starters."

Discussion Starters

1. Analyze Kelly's test scores to determine the nature and extent of her reading problem.

Grade Equivalent Conversion Tables
High Achievement Test

Raw Score	Level 12 VB	Level 12 RC	Level 13 VB	Level 13 RC	Raw Score
0	0.4	0.4	0.6	0.7	0
1	0.7	0.7	0.8	0.9	1
2	1.1	1.0	1.1	1.1	2
3	1.4	1.2	1.5	1.3	3
4	1.7	1.4	1.8	1.5	4
5	2.0	1.6	2.1	1.8	5
6	2.2	1.8	2.4	2.0	6
7	2.4	2.0	2.6	2.2	7
8	2.6	2.3	2.9	2.5	8
9	2.8	2.5	3.1	2.7	9
10	3.0	2.7	3.4	2.9	10
11	3.3	2.9	3.6	3.1	11
12	3.5	3.1	3.7	3.4	12
13	3.7	3.3	3.9	3.6	13
14	3.9	3.4	4.0	3.8	14
15	4.1	3.5	4.2	4.0	15
16	4.3	3.6	4.3	4.1	16
17	4.5	3.8	4.5	4.2	17
18	4.7	3.9	4.6	4.4	18
19	4.8	4.0	4.8	4.5	19
20	5.0	4.1	5.0	4.8	20
21	5.1	4.3	5.1	4.8	21
22	5.3	4.4	5.3	4.9	22
23	5.4	4.5	5.4	5.0	23
24	5.5	4.7	5.6	5.1	24
25	5.7	4.9	5.7	5.3	25
26	5.8	5.1	5.9	5.4	26
27	6.0	5.3	6.1	5.5	27
28	6.0	5.5	6.2	5.6	28
29	6.2	5.7	6.4	5.7	29
30	6.4	6.0	6.5	5.9	30
31	6.6	6.3	6.7	6.0	31
32			6.8	6.2	32
33			6.9	6.4	33
34			7.1	6.6	34
35			7.3	6.8	35
36			7.5	7.1	36
37			7.7	7.4	37
38			7.8	7.8	38
39					39
40					40
41					41
42					42
43					43
44					44
45					45
46					46
47					47
48					48
49					49
50					50

Grade Equivalent Conversion Tables
High Achievement Test

Raw Score	Level 14 VB	Level 14 RC	Level 15 VB	Level 15 RC	Raw Score
0	0.8	1.0	1.2	1.3	0
1	1.0	1.1	1.4	1.4	1
2	1.3	1.3	1.6	1.6	2
3	1.6	1.5	1.9	1.7	3
4	1.9	1.7	2.2	1.9	4
5	2.2	1.9	2.5	2.1	5
6	2.5	2.1	2.9	2.3	6
7	2.9	2.3	3.3	2.6	7
8	3.2	2.6	3.6	2.8	8
9	3.4	2.8	4.0	3.0	9
10	3.7	3.1	4.3	3.3	10
11	3.9	3.3	4.5	3.5	11
12	4.1	3.6	4.8	3.8	12
13	4.3	3.8	5.0	4.1	13
14	4.5	4.0	5.3	4.3	14
15	4.6	4.2	5.5	4.6	15
16	4.8	4.4	5.7	4.9	16
17	5.0	4.6	6.0	5.1	17
18	5.1	5.8	6.2	5.3	18
19	5.3	4.9	6.4	5.5	19
20	5.4	5.0	6.6	5.7	20
21	5.6	5.2	6.8	5.9	21
22	5.7	5.3	7.0	6.0	22
23	5.9	5.4	7.1	6.2	23
24	6.1	5.5	7.3	6.3	24
25	6.3	5.6	7.5	6.5	25
26	6.5	5.7	7.6	6.6	26
27	6.6	5.8	7.8	6.8	27
28	6.8	6.0	8.0	7.0	28
29	7.0	6.1	8.1	7.1	29
30	7.1	6.2	8.2	7.3	30
31	7.3	6.3	8.4	7.4	31
32	7.5	6.5	8.6	7.6	32
33	7.6	6.6	8.7	7.8	33
34	7.8	6.8	8.9	8.0	34
35	7.9	7.0	9.0	8.2	35
36	8.1	7.2	9.2	8.4	36
37	8.2	7.4	9.3	8.6	37
38	8.3	7.6	9.4	8.8	38
39	8.5	7.9	9.6	9.0	39
40	8.6	8.2	9.7	9.2	40
41	8.8	8.5	9.9	9.4	41
42	9.0	8.9	10.0	9.6	42
43	9.2	9.2	.10.1	9.9	43
44			10.3	10.1	44
45			10.5	10.4	45
46			10.6	10.6	46
47					47
48					48
49					49
50					50

Grade Equivalent Conversion Tables
High Achievement Test

Raw Score	Level 16 VB	Level 16 RC	Level 17 VB	Level 17 RC	Raw Score
0	1.4	1.8	1.7	2.3	0
1	1.6	1.9	1.9	2.4	1
2	1.8	2.0	2.1	2.5	2
3	2.1	2.1	2.4	2.6	3
4	2.4	2.2	2.7	2.7	4
5	2.7	2.3	3.0	2.8	5
6	3.1	2.6	3.4	3.0	6
7	3.5	2.8	3.9	3.3	7
8	4.0	3.1	4.4	3.7	8
9	4.4	3.4	4.8	4.1	9
10	4.7	3.7	5.2	4.5	10
11	5.0	4.1	5.5	4.9	11
12	5.4	4.4	5.8	5.2	12
13	5.7	4.8	6.2	5.6	13
14	6.0	5.1	6.5	6.0	14
15	6.3	5.5	6.7	6.3	15
16	6.5	5.8	7.0	6.6	16
17	6.8	6.0	7.3	6.9	17
18	7.0	6.3	7.5	7.1	18
19	7.2	6.5	7.8	7.4	19
20	7.4	6.7	8.0	7.6	20
21	7.6	6.9	8.2	7.8	21
22	7.8	7.1	8.4	8.0	22
23	8.0	7.3	8.6	8.1	23
24	8.2	7.4	8.8	8.3	24
25	8.4	7.5	9.0	8.5	25
26	8.5	7.8	9.1	8.6	26
27	8.7	7.9	9.3	8.7	27
28	8.8	8.1	9.5	8.9	28
29	8.9	8.2	9.6	9.0	29
30	9.1	8.4	9.8	9.2	30
31	9.2	8.5	10.0	9.3	31
32	9.4	8.6	10.1	9.5	32
33	9.5	8.8	10.3	9.7	33
34	9.7	9.0	10.5	9.9	34
35	9.8	9.1	10.7	10.1	35
36	10.0	9.3	10.9	10.3	36
37	10.2	9.5	11.1	10.5	37
38	10.3	9.7	11.3	10.7	38
39	10.4	9.9	11.4	11.0	39
40	10.6	10.1	11.6	11.2	40
41	10.8	10.3	11.8	11.5	41
42	10.9	10.6	11.9	11.8	42
43	11.0	10.8	21.2	12.0	43
44	11.2	11.0	12.2	12.2	44
45	11.3	11.2	12.4	12.4	45
46	11.5	11.4	12.6	12.6	46
47	11.7	11.6	12.8	12.8	47
48	11.9	11.9	12.9	12.9	48
49					49
50					50

14

Understanding Our Communication Challenge

14.1 "INCOMPLETE" GRADES GO OUT OF CONTROL

After much public debate, discussion with staff, and deliberation last year, your school board adopted a policy holding that teachers at your high school may not assign a grade of "F" unless they have assigned an "Incomplete" grade first. "Incomplete" means that the student has yet to complete all of the requirements for a course grade—that the work is still in progress and therefore it is misleading to conclude that the student has not learned the material. All the teacher can say is that the student has not yet demonstrated learning.

The policy requires that student and teacher agree on the work to be completed and set a date by which the student must deliver it. If the work is not done then, an "F" can be assigned.

The reason the board established this policy is to give students more time to learn. Consistent with a mastery learning model, the amount to be learned is held constant and the time allowed to learn it is free to vary. Variation in the pace of student learning is accommodated in this way. The messages the board wants to send are, "We value your learning whenever it happens," and "The more time spent learning, the more students will learn."

Now, some time later, however, the implications of such a policy are becoming clear and are the topic of discussion at your monthly faculty meeting. Here are some of the comments being offered by your colleagues:

"Many of my students have simply stopped working. They know I can't fail them—that they will get more time. So their motivation has disappeared."

"I've got a backlog of several dozen incompletes now. I have no idea when I will be able to evaluate them."

"Yeah, but I had one special needs student mainstreamed in my classroom who was convinced he could complete a key project if he just had more time. This policy saved him from a failing grade."

"Look, I'm a math teacher. Math unfolds as a series of prerequisites building on one another. No foundation, no new learning. Incompletes mean there is no foundation. What am I to do?"

Here's a different problem from the advanced placement science teacher: "I have B and C students who say they could complete the work to earn an A, given more time. Could I please give them an incomplete to buy them that time? They're right. And the result will be greater achievement on their part—definitely a good thing! When I say 'No, the incomplete is only for those in danger of failing,' they accuse me of denying them equal opportunity. What about the board's statement when it set the policy: 'We value learning whenever it happens'? Did they mean we value more learning among the failures only? No. But if my successful students had this option too, how could I possibly manage? What do we say to them?"

Obviously, a noble policy has given rise to some real classroom assessment and communication problems. Is this a bad policy or has it been implemented incorrectly?

Initial Reflections

1. How are students interpreting this policy? What does it mean to them—given their behavior?

2. How does this policy relate to student motivation to strive for academic excellence?

3. Under what conditions might this be a productive policy? A counterproductive policy?

Discussion Starters

1. Is their any hope for this policy? Can it be effective? If so, how?

2. If you were to remove this policy from the books, what justification would you give for doing so?

3. If you were to revise this policy or its implementation to maximize learning and minimize the problems identified above, how might you do that?

14.2 THE DISAPPEARING MOTIVATION

A Mom tells her story:

"When Mario first started school, he was so cute and so enthusiastic. He couldn't wait to get to class each day. He seemed to think so much of his teachers. He did very well academically, too. So did his friends from our neighborhood.

"But about 5th and 6th grade, things began to change. I can remember other moms beginning to ask the same thing: 'What happened? What changed?' At about 11 or 12 years old, our kids began to care less and less about school. Some parents attribute it to adolescence. They lose interest in academic things, what with hormones, girls, and all. But I don't buy that totally. Others think it's the teachers in those grades. But Mike's teachers seem to have been terrific. I think there must be more to it. Still other parents attribute the problem to the peer group. It's just not 'cool' to care about school. But I don't know. Mike has always been pretty independent. I just can't figure it out. We even took him to the doctor for a physical exam to see if he's OK. He is.

"The interesting thing is that the transition was slow: less homework to do or less time devoted to doing homework, more frequent expressions of frustration with his teachers, a growing sense of boredom with the whole enterprise. No teacher ever complained about Mario. But, you know, he just seemed to give up on himself. He began to think it was futile—he just couldn't do it. His grades slid gradually over a few years. He still isn't failing exactly, but his grades are low. And he's negative about school!

"At teacher conferences, they dismiss the problem. 'He's just going through a phase,' they say. 'He'll get past it and his grades will return to the top. He's such a smart boy.'

"When I ask them how they plan to motivate him in positive ways, they have no reply. All they say is, 'When he realizes what it's going to take to get into college, he'll straighten up.' But it may be too late by then. He'll be so far behind.

"I'm at my wits end. What should I do?"

Initial Reflections

1. What are some of the "academic" reasons for Mario's malaise? How might the classroom assessment, recordkeeping, and communication processes be contributing?

2. What might have motivated Mario academically in early grades? Why are those things not motivating him now?

3. How might you determine possible reasons for Mario's lack of motivation?

Discussion Starters

1. What might Mario's teachers do to rekindle the academic energy that burned within him several years earlier?

2. What information does his mom need to know about his progress to answer her concerns?

15

Developing Sound Report Card Grading Practices

15.1 THE DILEMMA OF THE ZERO

Your daughter is enrolled in a 10th grade biology course. The mid-term progress report sent home from school says she is getting a D+ in biology, yet the only tests and assignments you have seen have had A and B+ on the top. Your daughter reports having done all the required work and is at a loss to explain the grade. You request a meeting with the teacher.

At the meeting, you present the progress report, asking the teacher what it means. Without checking the record, the teacher reports that your daughter must not have been doing the work or the grade would be higher. He expresses disappointment when students don't measure up and complains about the lack of time to help students like your child—given that he faces 180 students per day. You begin to sense that this teacher isn't even sure who your daughter is.

You press the issue, asking to see her performance records. The teacher uses a computer grade book software program. He enters your daughter's name after asking you for the correct spelling and the screen shows a list of entries leading to an average of 69%. The teacher points out that the cutoff scores he has placed in the computer transforms this percentage into a D+. So the progress report is correct.

But as you scan the screen you notice the detailed list:

First unit test:	95%
Unit lab report:	85%
Second test:	85%
Unit lab report:	0%

You inquire about the 0%. If the report is missing, the computer is instructed to enter a zero into the record and into the computation of the grade. But, you point out, your child seems to be grasping the material very well and performing well on the required assessments. The teacher seems genuinely surprised at the reason for the low grade, agreeing that the rest of the record is very good. How is it, you ask, that the teacher concluded earlier that your child is not measuring up? The teacher retreats to the claim of having too little time to know every student.

Later, upon discussing the situation with your daughter, you find that she had specifically asked for permission to turn in the report late because she wanted to work on the data analysis on her home computer, and she was granted permission to do so. But the teacher has no recollection of that conversation.

Initial Reflections

1. Are the teacher's practices in this case sound from an assessment point of view? A communication point of view? A motivational point of view? The point of view of a beleaguered, overworked, over-committed teacher?

2. As a result of this conversation, your daughter's teacher is likely to remember her from now on. Is that a good or a bad thing? Is there reason to worry?

Discussion Starters

1. What action, if any, do you take? Does it involve the teacher? The teacher's supervisor? Your child?

2. Put yourself in this teacher's shoes. What might you have done to avoid this problem?

3. How can a parent take action to ensure the well-being of a child and still protect the integrity of the student's relationship with the teacher?

15.2 THE SERVICE TEACHER'S DILEMMA

Your district has a grading policy stipulating that students will receive a grade on their report cards for every subject they study every 10 weeks. There are no exceptions.

You are the district curriculum director—a former music teacher who left the classroom to provide leadership at a higher level. One day, after an all-faculty meeting in the high school auditorium, several teachers come to you asking for advice. They're all young teachers who have been told to come to you, both because of your position of authority and because you are "one of their kind." This phrase intrigues you! You sit down in the now empty auditorium to listen to their problem.

They're all elementary music, art, and P.E. teachers, with a librarian thrown in for good measure. Each has responsibility for providing instruction in three or four elementary schools. Thus each week, they face from 500 to 750 students. They see each student for what amounts to no more than a few minutes during any given grading period, and there are always 35 to 40 students present during their instruction.

Yet, they point out plaintively, they are forced to enter a grade on the report card of all students, the vast majority of whom they don't even know! High-quality assessment is out of the question, they point out, due to the lack of sufficient time. And even if they had time, they have no way of maintaining required performance records. Still further, even if they were to grade on effort alone, they have no way of knowing who is trying or not trying—let alone being able to connect such recollections to names on grade lists.

Your young staff members realize they are playing games with their grades in the name of appearing to have academic standards. They don't like it and they want your help.

Initial Reflections

1. Are the circumstances outlined by your teachers likely to have an impact on their ability to conduct assessments that meet the five key standards of assessment quality? Which standards will be affected and how?

2. Have any principles of effective grading been violated here? Which ones and how?

Discussion Starters

1. What do you say to these teachers? What actions do you urge them to take? What actions do you take—given your level of responsibility?

2. One teacher says she thinks that the best course of action may be to grade on the basis of effort alone and forget about student achievement. Is this a sound idea? What are its strengths? What might go wrong when it is put into practice?

15.3 THE STOLEN ANSWER KEY

A fifth grade teacher faces a dilemma. Several days ago, she was unable to come to work due to illness. As always, however, she was prepared for such last minute crises. Her lesson plans were in good order, so a substitute could pick up smoothly and carry on in her absence.

On this particular day, however, the substitute lacked some critical classroom management skills and things got out of hand. Although the principal was able to step in and quell the riot, the full implications of the disruption did not become apparent until several days later.

When our teacher returned, she continued her instruction as planned. In science class, she administered a unit test, a combination of multiple choice and short essay questions that went off without a hitch.

That afternoon as she scored the essays, she noticed a clear pattern in the responses of several students. Their answers were almost identical and the wording was similar to her model answer. Upon checking further, she found that each of these students had attained perfect scores on the multiple-choice portions of the tests—a level of performance she would have expected from only one of them. She suspected that the others had copied the test of her outstanding student. But how? She had no choice but to confront them.

As the teacher investigated, a very troubling realization began to emerge. The primary culprit was the star student; the others were co-conspirators. The substitute teacher had inadvertently left the answer key to the test on the desk during a pretest review and practice session. The outstanding student—who needed no help to ace this test—found it and saw an opportunity to win some friends. Desperate to be accepted as a peer, he copied the key and shared it with a few partners in crime. Thus the results witnessed by this teacher at test-scoring time.

Initial Reflections

1. Be sure to think broadly about the total picture presented here. What does the emergence of this behavior on the part of students say about the assessment environment in this classroom?

2. Are there affective or dispositional aspects of this scenario that deserve attention?

3. What are they and how might the teacher attend to them?

Discussion Starters

1. What actions should the teacher take in dealing with this situation?

2. What action should this teacher take with respect to the assessment of these students' achievement and the grades they receive—given what they did?

3. If punishment is warranted for the achievement hoax they perpetrated, what should that punishment be?

4. What should this teacher say to the parents of these students, if anything?

16

Using Portfolios as a Communication System

16.1 THE DILEMMA OF STUDENT SELECTION AND CLEAR COMMUNICATION

Portfolios have become part of the school-wide assessment system with some unexpected results. It's almost time for quarterly reporting. The teachers in this elementary school have enthusiastically embraced the notion of using portfolios as part of their assessment system. They've attended a portfolio workshop, spent time brainstorming and agreeing on portfolio purposes (showing growth over time, involving students in self-assessment, communicating more richly about student learning with parents, and having students involved in selecting and reflecting on their work). The PTA helped buy colorful portfolios for storing student products, and the staff developed sets of criteria for looking at certain kinds of work (problem solving, reading, and mathematics). But now that it's time to send the portfolios home, the results of the first round of student selection seem to be revealing some serious weaknesses:

"How can I send these portfolios home?" says one teacher, face to face with what she views as disaster. "Yesterday, I asked my students to make selections from their working folders. It seemed to go okay. Then I had them write brief reflections on why each piece was chosen. When I looked them over, I was horrified. They've chosen things that I never would have. Some of the most important work we've done all quarter isn't there. Parents will get a really poor picture of what we've been doing and what their children are learning. They're going to think we're not doing our jobs. And the reflections! The reasons are so trivial. 'I like it.' 'It got the best grade.' 'The colors are my favorites.' Where are their insights? They don't know what to say. I thought this portfolio idea was going to be the answer for us. Now I'm wondering if there's any way to salvage this mess."

"My students don't know how to make good selections," says another teacher. "I'm really not sure what to do now. Their thinking about it is very unsophisticated. I thought I had done a good job of helping them understand what a portfolio is all about, but it's obvious they don't have the same criteria in their heads that I have in mine. I value their involvement in the process, want them to feel ownership (this is supposed to be the story of their learning after all), but these portfolios just don't do the job."

A second grade teacher adds her thoughts: "I really did a lot to help them through the selection process. I even set up some pieces that had to be included—especially their unit books. After the first grade teachers tried it out, I decided to use their idea. We put together booklets that students make covers for and include the things they've done related to the unit. So everyone's portfolio includes some of the same stuff. Then they get to choose some other pieces. They're still not very good at reflection, but I'm a little bit more secure about sending things home now. Still, there are things that are really important that I don't know how to deal with, like group projects and things they construct. I'm also starting to worry about whether we're going to need a whole new building to house the portfolios at the end of the year—never mind next year!"

One of the upper grade teachers mentions his concern that the portfolios don't really let parents see the things they expect to find out about; samples of problem solving are great, but what about showcasing science, health, social studies? "Do you think we need to have separate portfolios for each subject area? But that would defeat our decision to help students build connections across disciplines and our emphasis on thematic learning and interdisciplinary curriculum."

In frustration and with worries about changes in their own thinking about portfolios, the group asks for a chunk of time on the next faculty meeting agenda. There are questions inside of questions that need to be examined: Should we all send home portfolios? Can we individually choose not to? Since we've spent so much time on portfolios, how will we come up with other information for parents if we don't use them? Formal reporting is just around the corner and something has to be decided.

Initial Reflections

1. What actions do you think were taken to prepare students for selecting among their work samples?

2. What do you think about the dilemma of balancing student selection and accurate communication about learning?

3. Do you have experiences that can contribute to solutions for this case?

Discussion Starters

1. Do you see some underlying questions about the student's role in portfolios that need to be answered here?

2. How do you feel about student self-selection? Why?

3. Is there a way to salvage this situation? What actions could the teachers take?

4. Are there any advantages to sending the portfolios home as they are? What are the risks? What would you do? Why?

5. If you did recommend sending the portfolios home, what additional information, if any, would you include? Why?

6. What changes should the teachers make if they continue using portfolios?

16.2 PORTFOLIO REFLECTIONS: HOW DO WE JUDGE QUALITY?

You have agreed to serve on a committee to develop a set of performance criteria to evaluate the quality of student self-reflections. In preparation for your work, teachers in your district have selected material from their student portfolios that includes student reflections on the quality of their work. These samples cross elementary grade levels and subjects, including math, reading, and writing. Your work unfolds in stages, each of which presents its own unique set of challenges.

Stage 1: The Focus of Reflections

As you begin to review the students' reflections on the quality of their work, you find that there are inconsistencies in the things students write about, so you ask to see the writing instructions these teachers gave. One assignment reads like this:

1. Look at your work. What did you learn? (Use action words)

2. What did you do really well?

3. What do you need to improve?

Another teacher presented this assignment:

1. What does this work show about your learning? Why did you pick this work?

2. How good do you think this work is and why?

A third teacher took a different approach:

1. How good is this work and why?
2. What does it say about how your work is changing over time?

A member of your team asks, "Can we use student responses to these different assignments to develop a common set of performance criteria? These students were reflecting and writing about fundamentally different things."

Discussion Starters

1. Is this teacher correct? Are generic criteria possible, given these differing instructions?
2. What might those common criteria look like? Collect your initial thoughts about them before moving on.

Stage 2: Drafting Some Criteria

Your team decides to move ahead. You divide into subcommittees to examine student self-reflections within the three subjects. Then you plan to pool your criteria across subjects, again to see if generic criteria can be developed. You opt to work with the math committee. Your group begins by sorting student self-reflections into piles according to your perceptions of quality. After sorting, you review and discuss reflections you consider "excellent," striving to find descriptive language to capture their essence. Then you consider "adequate" and "poor" levels of self-reflection. From these, you devise this five-point rating scale:[1]

ASSIGN A RATING OF 5 WHEN:

Reasons for selection are given and elaborated; specific reference is made to mathematics and to standards; quality is judged; reasons are clear and insightful; reflection reveals a knowledge of standards and is thoughtful.

ASSIGN A RATING OF 4 WHEN:

Reasons are elaborated; there is some specific reference to math; judgments are made about quality; there is some insight into learning; the reflection may refer to standards.

ASSIGN A RATING OF 3 WHEN:

Reasons are clear; math terms are used, the reasons make sense; there is little elaboration; the quality of the work is not directly addressed or is addressed in a way that is general and repetitious.

ASSIGN A RATING OF 2 WHEN:

Some awareness of the math is involved; there is limited description; there is almost no elaboration or use of examples; there is limited description of quality; remarks are general.

ASSIGN A RATING OF 1 WHEN:

The reflection is very general; there is no elaboration; the writing sometimes refers to the effort used, not the math; no judgments are made, judgments like "good" or "OK" are given with no evidence offered, or the reflection mostly describes the effort the student made.

Discussion Starters

1. Do you think this rating scale can serve as the basis for sound evaluation of student self-reflections? Are there changes you might suggest?
2. Do you think the rating scale can provide a basis for the development of generic performance ratings—for use with other subjects?

Stage 3: Comparing Notes

Now the group working with student reflections in the area of writing reports on the results of its work and offers this rating scale:

STRONG

Shows understanding of the criteria (the school's vision, the writing criteria), and elaborates on reasons for making certain selections.

This elaboration can include parts of the student's selections.

The student connects selections to own purposes; own meaning.

The student provides specific examples.

The student make statements about improvement—what's been learned and what can be applied to another task.

DEVELOPING

The student is beginning to apply criteria but only in a general way.

There is a sense of discovery but few statements of elaboration or support are given.

NOT YET

No explanation is provided.

Reflection is overly general and vague.

Reflection is a comment on the topic or activity rather than on the big idea/capability like writing.

Reflection is a summary of the assignment/task.

The focus is on appearance; neatness.

Comments are not supported with references that match the writing criteria.

Then the group evaluating student self-reflections in reading chimes in with its proposal:[2]

STRONG

Several (or more) of the self-reflections show thoughtful consideration of personal strengths and needs based on an in-depth understanding of the criteria. These reflections may also include statements of personal goals; responses to learning, to the unit of study, or to an assignment; summaries of growth over time; or other insights regarding the individual story this student's work tells.

DEVELOPING

Self-reflections provide at least a superficial analysis of strengths and needs, which may or may not be tied to specific criteria for judging performance or growth. Students may include comments on what they like or dislike about the content arena or unit of study, or about what they find difficult or challenging; but the reflections may not include insights regarding growth, needs, goals, or changes in performance over time.

NOT YET

Self-reflections are rudimentary: e.g. "I like it." "It took be a long time to do." "My teacher liked it." No reference is made to criteria.

This group adds to its report the caution that these students were only in their first year of self-reflection. They had not received a great deal of instruction on how to do it well. So the high end of their scale—of all the scales—might not be high enough next year and the year after, as skills improve. The implication, they point out, is that whatever scale they develop will have to be reviewed and revised on a regular basis.

Discussion Starters

1. Do you think it is a good idea to develop generic criteria in this case across grade levels? Across subjects? Why or why not?

2. Which is likely to be most useful in this situation: a holistic scale or analytical ratings?

3. If you were to go for holistic and created it by merging these three scales, what might your resulting rating scale look like? Create a draft version of it.

4. If you were to develop analytical rating scales, what dimensions would you include? How would you define each? What might the scales look like? Create draft versions.

5. As a team, if you were asked to offer suggestions for how to help students deepen their evaluations of their own work, what specific ideas would you offer?

16.3 A REQUEST FROM HIGH PLACES

It's the end of the day and you have found a few quiet minutes at your desk to reflect on the day and to begin to get ready for tomorrow. The phone rings. It's your supervisor asking for your help with a problem.

It seems that the education committee of your state senate has been advised that portfolios are the trend of the future in the schools of your state. So the chair of the committee is crafting a bill to place before the senate requiring that schools assemble a portfolio for every student. Your district has established a reputation as the state leader in the development of portfolios, so the senator is bringing her key staff members with her to a meeting at the district office next week to solicit your advice on the bill's content.

Not only does your supervisor not have the portfolio background to lead that meeting, he will be out of town that day and wants you to take over. You are the one the senator will count on to advise her about crafting this legislation. Your challenge is to prepare your presentation for the meeting.

Initial Reflections

1. Has the senator been given sound advice regarding this legislation? Is it a good idea?
2. What is motivating this legislation? What do you think might be her purposes for proposing this bill?
3. How should the issue of portfolio purpose play out in this legislation?
4. Whose concerns might need to be addressed in this case and how might they be addressed?

Discussion Starters

1. What topics will you cover at this meeting and how will you cover them?
2. Might you involve the senator in an actual examination of student portfolios? Why or why not? If so, how?

NOTES

[1]Adapted from Waialae Elementary School, Honolulu, Hawaii. Work in progress. Used by permission.

[2]Adapted from a rubric developed by Vicki Spandel and Ruth Culham, Northwest Regional Educational Laboratory, Portland, Oregon 1993. Used by permission.

17

Tapping the Full Potential of Student-Involved Communication

17.1 THE SPECIAL NEEDS STUDENT REVISITED

Return to case 2.3, Assessing Special Needs Students, reread the case description, and review your response. Now that you have completed your study of student-centered assessment, student-involved recordkeeping, and student-involved communication, what additional advice would you give Matthew's mom in dealing with the dilemma she spelled out?

17.2 THE HIGH SCHOOL FACULTY DEBATE ON STUDENT-LED CONFERENCES

A high school principal has just returned from a national conference on assessment full of excitement about an innovative new idea—student-led parent conferences—and he has put the topic on the agenda for the next faculty meeting. After introducing it to his colleagues and discussing some of its positive aspects, the principal invites the faculty to comment.

As it turns out, a teacher has had some experience with this strategy at his previous school. There, students assembled portfolios that included all subjects and met with their parents in home room at year's end to review their achievement. Conferences were 20 minutes, so it took a long day and an evening to complete them all.

For this teacher, such conferences just didn't work. First of all, 20 minutes was not enough to cover six different subjects. (That's about 3 minutes per subject to review a year's worth of achievement.) Further, students didn't know what work to place in their portfolios or how to share it, so the meetings turned out to be very brief discussions of the report card grades—completely from the student's point of view. That much could have been accomplished in the traditional setting—at home. Besides, homeroom teachers were not equipped to answer parents' questions in subjects other than their own, so parents' needs were not satisfied and they remained unimpressed—especially given the time they had invested. All in all, student reporting was a disaster and was abandoned after one try.

Another teacher offers a different experience. She had one student who seemed full of academic potential but didn't seem to care about school. Her older siblings had done very well in high school, but she herself was just not invested. At one point, the teacher had tried to find out why. The only reply she got was, "If my parents don't care, why should I?"

The teacher called the student's parents to discuss the matter. Suffice it to say, there had been a severe breakdown in communication in the family. In a risky move, the teacher bet the student that her parents did care and that she could prove it. During the next grading period, the two of them assembled a growth portfolio showing the student's improvement. This was not a general requirement—it was just for this student this term. Further, the teacher asked her to think about how she might present herself as an improving student and to write biweekly self-reflections about the work in her portfolio. As the term ended, the teacher requested the student to invite her parents in for a special parent/teacher conference. The surprise was that she asked her student to conduct that meeting, presenting herself as an able and growing learner.

The conference was a success for all; communication barriers (and even some emotional barriers) came down and the student found both a caring family and some new motivation to try. The teacher hastens to add that she couldn't do it for all or even most of her students. But for a few, when used carefully, she says, student-led conferences can make the difference. "Don't reject this idea out of hand," she warns.

In response to these comments, the principal makes a proposal: The faculty could institute student-led conferences to address three priorities. First, twelfth graders are required to complete special senior projects. Second, the guidance staff has all college-bound students assemble hypothetical "college admissions portfolios" to help them prepare for the application process. Third, students are required to complete a certain number of community service hours during their high school years and assemble evidence of the productivity of their work. All three, he suggests might provide an excellent basis for a school and community-wide, end-of-year acknowledgment of a productive school year.

Specifically, he proposes a three-day "Annual School Success Celebration" to provide a basis for student-involved conferences of various types. Senior projects might culminate in "show case" conferences in which students present their work for review and discussion. These conferences would involve families and local community representatives. College admissions portfolios might be shared with parents or review boards that could include some college admissions officers. Or students might develop growth portfolios from their community service experiences. Most conferences would center on individual students, but some group presentations might be in order. Perhaps an evening of artistic, musical, theatrical, and athletic accomplishments could serve as the culmination of the celebration. No awards—just accomplishments.

The principal asks for volunteers to see if this is feasible.

Initial Reflections

1. What may be motivating the principal here?
2. Is his celebration a good idea from the teachers' perspective?
3. Is it a good idea from the students' point of view?
4. Is it a good idea from the community's point of view?

Discussion Starters

1. Make a 2 x 2 chart, crossing students and teachers on one dimension with benefits and problems on the other. Use it to analyze pluses and minuses from each point of view. Based on your analysis, is this a good idea?
2. Based on your evaluation, make a detailed recommendation to the principal detailing (a) why it's a bad idea or (b) if you feel it's workable, what resources must be brought to bear to make it work.

17.3 THE FAILED CONFERENCE

Brad, a sixth grade student, is prepared for the conference in which he will show his "progressfolio." He has his agenda written out and has selected work samples from his notebooks. The day before the student-teacher-parent conference is scheduled, the teacher provides time for role plays. All the students take turns being the teacher, the parents, or the student. It's a noisy, busy time in the class. As the students leave at the end of the day, the teacher asks each one, "Are you ready for your conference?" Almost all say yes except for Lisa and later Brad. Lisa explains that her mom has new twins and might not be able to come. The teacher nods and says that they can hold the conference another time if it turns out that Lisa's mom can't come. "Don't make her feel bad about it, Lisa. Tell her we'll reschedule. I can always come out to your house!"

When Brad arrives at the door, he explains that his dad might have to go out of town and that his little brother is sick. "Not to worry," says the teacher, "we'll figure something out if that happens. By the way, did you bring your self-evaluation back?"

"Ahh, no. I was going to but Dad wanted to read it through again."

"Tomorrow then. Right, Brad? I need that back."

"Okay, I'll get it." Brad heads to his locker.

The next day is a busy one. The teacher has 27 conferences scheduled. Parents arrive. In each conference, parents and child spend 20 to 30 minutes reviewing the term's work, listening to the child read a passage, and hearing about math learned.

The participants review strengths, discuss areas needing improvement, and set goals for the coming term. It's an invigorating process. The parents are positive, and there's lots of work to show—even the kids are surprised by how much they have accomplished during the term.

About 2:40 Brad appears at the door with his dad. The teacher glances up and smiles. Brad looks nervous. That happens, she thinks; he's a good student, always tries hard, and has lots to show for it. She returns her focus to the conference under way.

Next time she glances up, Brad and his dad are busy looking at his materials. Brad's dad is gesturing as he talks. He seems to be asking lots of questions and is pretty animated. That's common enough, but Brad's not smiling. He's looking around as if he's wondering who's able to hear.

"I never did get that self-evaluation back," the teacher remembers. Finishing up the conference in which she's involved, she heads over to where Brad and his dad are meeting, greets him warmly, and introduces herself.

"Well, have you had a chance to show your dad your work Brad?"

Brad nods and his dad says, "I have some questions about Brad's work."

"Why don't we sit down and continue?"

She sits down across from Brad and his dad and begins with her standard opening question to the parents, "Is there any question you'd really like to have answered before this conference is over?"

"Yes, as a matter of fact there is. I would like to know why Brad is doing the same work as last year. It looks to me like he hasn't learned anything. He's really lazy at home but I don't let him get away with it. He's really bamboozled you! What kind of teacher are you?"

Taking a deep breath the teacher looks at Brad's dad and says, "So you're not sure Brad is learning enough to get him ready for next year?"

"Yes. And, I don't think you're doing your job. Brad brings home work he's evaluated himself or that another student has evaluated. Don't you mark anything? And look, he did a report on *The Motorcycle Rider*. He read that two years ago."

"So, you have concerns about Brad's instructional program?"

"Darn right."

"Okay. Let's get started with the conference and then when we're done, you and I can spend a few minutes talking about Brad and his program. I'm going to ask Brad and then you to describe Brad's strengths. Then we'll talk about the areas that need improvement, and finally we'll set some goals. Brad, can you begin by telling us three things you do really well?"

"I'm really good at math. I score high on all my tests, and other kids come and ask me for help."

"See, that's what I mean," says Brad's dad interrupting, "Why is Brad helping the other kids? Why aren't you? It's not Brad's job. You're getting the paycheck!"

"Excuse me. We need to have Brad's conference before we talk about the issues you raised. Brad, what's another area of strength?"

Brad describes two more areas he does well and shows his dad the evidence.

Brad's dad sits looking unhappy. Brad's teacher turns to him and says, "Can you tell Brad three things he does really well?"

"Yeah, I can but this is stupid. Brad doesn't need to know this stuff. He needs to know that his job is to stop being lazy and get to work. This is what's wrong with schools today."

The teacher interrupts, "Mr. Smith, it seems as though you don't want to have this conference. Could I suggest we just stop now and schedule a time when you and I can meet and talk about your concerns?"

"No. I took time off work and came in today and you haven't answered my questions yet. I don't want to come back again. I'm busy earning a living. I can't be coming in here all the time."

"I have another conference scheduled in five minutes. Let's go to the office and speak with the principal. You have concerns about my classroom program and I think it is important that we discuss them." She stands. "Let's go and make an appointment right now. Brad, why don't you wait in the library? There's a book sale on today."

Brad's dad shakes his head. "No, Brad. Come with me. We have to get going."

The teacher walks to the office wondering if she'll be able to get Brad's dad to make an appointment. He seems intent on leaving. The principal is standing in the hall greeting parents as they walk by. The teacher signals to him and then briefly outlines the fact that Brad's dad has some serious concerns and that there needs to be a meeting but she has other parents waiting. Brad's dad begins to shake his head in protest, but the principal begins to ask questions of him. Brad's dad turns to listen. The teacher smiles at Brad trying to reassure him and leaves wondering what the heck that was all about. Taking a deep breath, she returns to her next conference.

Initial Reflections

1. What went wrong?
2. Could this interaction have been anticipated? Could it have been avoided? If so, how?

Discussion Starters

1. What could the teacher have done to prevent this kind of conference? What else could the teacher have done to deal with the situation?
2. What should the teacher say to the student in the aftermath? To the parent?
3. Should the principal be involved in a further meeting?